Of Myself

RABINDRANATH
TAGORE
Of Myself
(ATMAPARICHAY)

Translated from Bengali by
DEVADATTA JOARDAR
and
JOE WINTER

ANVIL PRESS POETRY

Published in 2006
by Anvil Press Poetry Ltd
Neptune House   70 Royal Hill   London SE10 8RF
www.anvilpresspoetry.com

Translation, introduction and notes
copyright © Devadatta Joardar and Joe Winter 2006

This book is published
with financial assistance from
Arts Council England

Set in Monotype Fournier by Anvil
Printed and bound in England
by Cromwell Press, Trowbridge, Wiltshire

ISBN 0 85646 389 2

A catalogue record for this book
is available from the British Library

This edition is not for sale in the SAARC area

The surprising thing is this, I am coming to be,
I am finding expression.

RABINDRANATH TAGORE

Contents

Introduction

RABINDRANATH TAGORE died in 1941 in the family home in Calcutta where he had been born eighty years before. Many alive now recall the event. The death was not unexpected but the shock to Bengal was seismic. It was a life that belonged to Bengal and beyond, to India and beyond, to the world and beyond – to creation. A distance of more than sixty years may not yet be enough for a full picture to settle. But we are at a juncture, perhaps, when Tagore has outlived his labels and his life and work can emerge in a fresh light. "Romantic poet", "Upanishadic sage", "Baul", with other terms both more and less flattering, have tended to obscure the view. These few essays, first published as a collection in 1943, tell something of the man. The inner sight that directed the outer life is revealed, to a degree; so that we have, if not an autobiography, then the essence of it.

The outer life – what he did, what he manifestly was – as lives go was extraordinary. An excellent account in English is *Rabindranath Tagore: a Biography* by Krishna Kripalani (first published by Oxford University Press, London and Grove Press, New York in 1962). Tagore's writings are abundant and prodigiously expressive, yet free from the strain of effort and self-consciousness. His poetry is unequalled in lyric scope and variety. His novels, short stories, dramas of prose and verse and dance, and his penetrating essays and studies on a vast array of topics, are all informed by the springs of a great poetic mind. His more than two thousand songs form a unique branch of Indian music. They are among his finest poetry. In later life he turned his hand to painting and is seen as one of those who took Indian art into

9

the modern world. All this was only a part of the man and indeed only a part of the poet. He was an educationalist (founding and teaching at a school and university), a social activist, a nationalist and internationalist alike. In this last respect he was ahead of the time and perhaps still is. There is more to be said of his reforming spirit, that touched on matters large and small, so that life seemed almost to take in him a new direction; and yet to say more is not to the present purpose. The outer life in a sense is incidental to the inner vision. In these six pieces, written at widely differing intervals over his later decades, we are close to Rabindranath Tagore at his most introspective.

The first piece came out in a collection called *Bangabhashar Lekhak* ("Writers of the Bengali Language") in 1904. Tagore had been asked to write an account of himself and responded significantly. Later he was twice to publish a more conventional autobiographical sketch, each on his early life. They are charming and at times moving, but far removed from the search for a defining statement of the poet in him, that he now undertook. Later, too, he was to complain that what was written about his life missed the point. "Where is the poet?" He is here, and in the succeeding pieces, all of which, on their various occasions, carry the response of a writer's soul.

The title strikes a fine balance between inner and outer. *Atmaparichay* is literally "self-introduction" and more naturally "of myself". Tagore is always accessible; if he speaks of inward matters he is not esoteric; and the collection is important precisely in that it brings something hidden into the public domain. The account by one man of a poetic vocation is authentic.

He is one of the great prose-writers too, by the standards of any language. Even before his poetry was to mature, he wrote prose with a precocious majesty, wit and composure. It was in his hands that Bengali was to pass into the modern age and the written and spoken word fuse into a usable form of excellence. Able to explore the horizons of language both in prose and verse, he seems to have felt acutely what lay beyond expression. He was to pronounce in a late poem that he would depart with "the dishonour of unflowered utterance" upon him. It is perhaps from the sense of an area beyond knowing, where words fall short, that Tagore drew his primal certainties.

There is a discussion in the first piece of *jibandebata*. Literally "life-god", the word was Tagore's own and the concept of deep importance to him. (He quotes from a poem of his of that title.) It resists definition, yet may in part be said to be a guiding presence in life, to be discovered in ever-new revelation. In the third piece, that is specifically to do with his religion, he finds no need for the word. One has to be careful of the facile use of words and ideas in considering Tagore; for as he makes clear he eschewed the "secondary injunctions" of religion and its easy labels. He is a humanist rooted in the Brahmo faith (a breakaway movement from traditional Hinduism) and in the Vedas and Upanishads of Sanskrit scripture. But as he wrote to a friend, "Can you squeeze me behind any one religious boundary?" In these essays, seeking to present something of the self, he refers naturally to what is familiar and personal to him, to his poetry, to several Sanskrit *slokas*, and at one point to *jibandebata*. The Bengali verses that he quotes, all his own, are central to the discussion. In translating them care has been taken to preserve the structural balance; and to allow the lyric impulse to add its freshness to the meaning. Perhaps one can see the poet's religion as a river that never ceased to nourish the creative ground. In speaking of it he uses the idea of a personal Being and the translators regret their use of He for the pronoun: Bengali is able to stay neutral in the matter. Any other use in English is forced after a time, which is not what the author would have wished.

The second piece, that touches on a poet's rewards, was read out by Tagore at a public meeting held in honour of his fiftieth birthday. It was published in the periodical *Bharati* later that year (1911). The third was in reply to a critical review of his religious beliefs. It was published in the periodical *Sabuj Patra* in 1917. The fourth was an address at another birthday function, his seventieth, and printed in the periodical *Prabasi* in 1931. The fifth was in response to a vast public recognition of the same event, read out to a gathering of students at the Senate Hall in Calcutta and printed in a booklet called *Pratibhashan* ("Reply"). The final piece appeared as he entered his eightieth year and came out in *Prabasi* in 1940. It was written at Santiniketan.

If literature was a focus for his inner energies the village of Santiniketan was where Tagore's practical life sought an ideal. In the deepest of ways he lived his life for his people. From 1901, when he started a school there, to his death, he worked continuously to let the creative currents of society find their freedom. In the closing passage of the final piece in this collection he is talking of the school, where lessons still are taken in the open. Santiniketan still has a touch of the forest retreat. The name means "quiet haven" and the various endeavours the poet gave himself to in its locality have woven themselves into its soul. The university Tagore founded there in 1918, that he named Visva-Bharati, was a meeting-place for East and West. The name suggests an academy with the world and India at one and it drew lecturers from far and near. It remains a point of creative outreach and exchange. A many-tiered movement for development in local villages that the poet set in being still stands as a way forward. To all these projects a sense of Nature was critical; and he worked mightily for them all. But the school was always at his heart.

Atmaparichay is the rarest of personal records. It is an honest dealing with the poet's deepest aspirations. In a somewhat fortuitous progression its pages present an engagement with life in the years of maturity. A heart of love, a mind at its service that can cut like a knife, and in some sense the spirit of a child are here. In all his many and varied original works Rabindranath lives again. In this, the first English translation of a journey that seems to go to the source of discovery itself, it is hoped that the breath of a child of the Earth is not lost.

WE DEDICATE this translation to the memory of Devadas Joardar and of Jacob Miller.

We wish to thank Shyamasree Lal, Susmita Bhattacharya, Buddhajiban Chakrabarti, Subhas Choudhury and Sankha Ghosh for their generous assistance.

DEVADATTA JOARDAR
JOE WINTER

Calcutta 2006

Of Myself

I

I HAVE BEEN asked to write an account of my life. I do not intend to waste space being unnecessarily modest, but it should be said at the outset that the special gift for autobiography belongs to special people, and not to me. Nothing will be lost, however, as I see no profit to anyone in a detailed description of my life.

And so from my life-account I omit the account. I shall simply try to describe fairly briefly how my life has found expression through poetry. For the vanity in this I earnestly beg to be forgiven by my readers.

When I look back on this process of my writing poetry for so long I can see this clearly – it's a business over which I have had no control. When I was writing, I thought, it is I who am writing, but now I know that's not true. Because these poems are fragments and in them the significance of the whole body of the poetry is incomplete. And what that significance was I had no idea. I had been adding one poem to another, blind to the consequence. The little meaning of each one I imagined I saw at a given point. Now taking them as a whole I see well enough that a single continuous significance flowed through them all. And so many years later I wrote,

> *Say what ever-new jest is this,*
> *mistress of life's jests, I pray?*
> *Say what space you will allow*
> *for the words that I would say?*
> *To the soul's depths you attach:*
> *and language from the mouth you snatch,*

and so my words you match, re-match,
  in your own song's way.
What I want to say is gone,
I say what you insist upon,
as down song's river I float on,
  lost and far away.

I see that a rule of the cosmic order will not permit what is present, and what is imminent, a dwarfish status. It will not allow it to know it is merely one of a series of steps. It tells it that it is sufficient in itself. When the flower blooms, it seems the tree's one object and aim is the flower itself. Such is its beauty, its fragrance, that in its wealth it appears the all and sum of the forest goddess's devotions. That it is merely an anticipation of the fruit's fruition, remains a secret – it rejoices in the magnificence of the present, it is not to be outshone by the future. Again it seems, looking at the fruit, this is the acme of fruitfulness; but that the future tree's seed is maturing in the womb stays well hidden. In this way Nature, by preserving the ultimate quality of the flower within the flower, and of the fruit within the fruit, lets a consequence that is beyond them proceed unnoticed by them.

Regarding the composition of poetry we see the same cosmic law – at least within myself I have felt its presence. In the act of writing something I have felt the piece was the end in itself. And so in the process of completing it I have been sustained by a great care and delight. That I am writing it, and that in writing it I am resorting to a particular emotion, cannot be denied. But now I know all that writing is merely the occasion: every piece is building up something that is yet to come, something it has not the faintest idea of. Inside the author is again an author, before whom the future significance is visibly present. Through the several airholes of a flute the breath awakens a number of melodies and loudly proclaims its own control; yet who is turning the melody-fragments into a *ragini*? Certainly the breath is awakening the tunes, and yet the breath is not playing the flute. To the player all *ragas* and *raginis* are present and living, there is nothing that is hidden from him.

> *By the door, at the room's side,*
> *I spoke to someone close beside;*
> *so many tales I could confide*
> *   of my own ways and world...*
> *but all my words you give to the fire*
> *or launch on tears, to sink, expire...*
> *by a new means, to your desire,*
> *   an image new you build.*

I suppose the meaning of this verse is this, that what I am about to write is a little matter, nothing much at all – and then a tune is visited on these words of mine such that a simple matter is made a large one, and rather than being personal it is of the wider world. The tune itself was not a part of my intention. On my sheet I was sketching a drawing, in it a colour blossomed – and the colour and the colour-brush were not in my hands at all.

> *A new blind rhythm runs along*
> *in its delight; and a new song*
> *fills out a pain that sounds out strong.*
> *   A singing word*
> *I have not thought, I have not planned...*
> *a pain wakes I don't understand.*
> *For whom this message, from whose hand?*
> *   I have not heard.*

When a certain trifling personage, myself, took a whim to make some trifling statement or other, someone would exclaim in fervent support, "Go on, say it, say what you have to say! Everyone's desperate to hear your words!" With this he would look at the audience and wink. He would smile a little with a kindly humour and through my words arrange to say his own, whatever it is they were.

Who knows what it is all about?
Some say this or that beyond doubt –
some seek me in vain, to question me out –
you must laugh at the view.
Who are you – where are you hiding out?
I die looking for you.

Is it only that in poetry-writing a certain agent is going beyond the poet and operating the pen? I do not think so. For together with that I have come to see that while life is being moulded, someone is weaving all its joys and sorrows, its pluses and minuses in their fragmentary process into a continuous significance. Whether I have always acted in the interests of this being or not I don't know; but in my dangers, in my difficulties, he is knitting up all the damage I undergo, piecing it together, shoring it up. And not only that: my instincts and self-interest limit my life, confine it to a certain meaning; but he is continually ripping up the limit – and through deep pain and severance of ties, he is fusing it with what is immense and what is great and cosmic. When one day life stepped out into the market it did not look for fulfilment in the arena of universal humankind – it had been saving its cowrie-shells for the comfort and prosperity of the home. But from that earthy path, the sad and glad domestic way, who is forcibly dragging it off, out past hills and mountains and valleys and plateaus?

Say what ever-new jest is this,
mistress of life's jests, I pray?
The traveller wants that way or this –
but do you let him find his way?
The village path the village shows:
farmers come back at day's close,

cows trot to the field, a housewife goes
        for water, all in their turn ...
once at the very first hour of day
I went out carefree on that way.
I thought all day I'd work and play
        and at night return.
But you confuse all my steps so,
the way for sure I cannot know.
Bewildered, weary as I go,
        a strange land here I see.
Now I tread a hill-top high,
now in pain's dark cave I lie ...
as like a madman I go by
        a way not known to me.

This poet who takes up all the good and bad in me, all my constituent parts, the favourable and unfavourable alike, to go on creating my life – it is he that in my poetry I call "Jibandebata". I do not believe that he is merely giving a unity to the fragmentariness of my present life, allowing it to be in harmony with the world. From time immemorial and through any number of forgotten situations, I know he has brought me to the expression of the present moment. An immense memory of a long sequence of existence continuing through this world has gathered round him, and lies in me, in my unconscious. That is why I can feel a kinship of such long standing with the world's flora and fauna. That is why the huge mysterious world does not seem alien and terrible.

Today it seems, in midst of all
        I have held you dear.
Adrift for ever in humankind,
        just you and I are here.
        As I gaze on every side,
        something wakens deep inside ...
as if everywhere, you and I

are endlessly allied.
So many eras in the skies
    I spent — still to forget
the light that trembles in the stars,
    where you and I sway yet.

When upon the Earth I look
    in Ashwin's new light,
and see the grass-enchantment there,
    I thrill in delight.
        It seems that in me I have heard
        a never-to-be-spoken Word ...
within the heart of this dumb world,
    the feeling that is stirred.
Within the life-rich earth we two
    such eras have let pass,
in so many autumns' golden light
    have trembled in the grass. ...

The dawn that millions of years ago
    upon the planet rose
in sunbeam-particles — do you
    not weave my life with those?
        But where and when was my dawn's hour?
        Hiding in my life your power,
amid what images of yours
    did you make me flower?
Eternal old one, still again,
    again, you fashion me.
You were ever at my side,
    ever you will be.

I have no special claim to knowledge of philosophy. If there is a debate about, say, monism and dualism, I will not respond. I am speaking solely from the standpoint of feeling. Within me is the happiness of an expression of my inner god – that joy and that love have flooded my limbs and senses, my mind and intellect, this universe right in front of me, my past without beginning and my future without end. Certainly I understand nothing of this play of love, and yet it is always taking place within me. The light that pleases my eyes, the cloud-glow of dawn and dusk that pleases, the greenery of grass and foliage that pleases, the image of a loved one's face that pleases – all this is a succession of waves brimming with love's divine play. And within it frolic the shadows of the whole of life, joy and sorrow, light and dark.

Within me between what is being built up and the one who is building is an affinity of joy, a bond of eternal love; and if through all the events of life this is witnessed and understood, then in the midst of joy and sorrow peace is at hand. When I feel he has drawn to himself the overflowing expression of my every joy, and has himself accepted all my grief and pain, then I know that nothing at all has been in vain, all is blessed in the light of a world-encompassing fullness.

Here I quote part of an old letter of mine –

"I can by no means say that I have been able to acquire within myself, in a clear and strong form, what is usually spoken of as religion. But I can often feel that in the depths of my mind something living is being created. It is no kind of particular dogma – but a deep consciousness, a new organ of my soul. I can see clearly that gradually I shall be able to find an internal consistency and harmony – that taking together all my happiness and unhappiness, my inside and outside, my beliefs and behaviour, I shall be able to give a completeness to life. I cannot say whether what is written in the scriptures is true or false; but all such truth is quite unsuited to me; in fact it could be said that for me it has no existence for much of the time. What I shall be able to build up with the whole of my life is my ultimate truth. When I feel the joys and sorrows of life in a momentary, fragmented manner,

I cannot rightly understand the endless mystery of a creative process within us – as when one has to spell out every word, one cannot understand the meaning and unity of emotion of an entire passage of poetry. But when the unbroken strand of unity of the creative power within oneself can once be felt, I can realise my own link with the endlessly created universe; I can see how the planets and stars, the moon and sun are being created in their constant burning and circling. Just so in me from time without beginning a process of creation has been going on. Within it my joy and sorrow, desire and pain accept their respective places. What will come out of this I don't know, since we don't even know what a speck of dust is. But when I look at my own flowing life in its connection with the infinite world and time outside itself, then I can see all life's sorrows tied to a huge strand of happiness – I exist, I become, I continue, I can understand this is a large affair, I am and with me everything else also is, not even a molecule or an atom of this endless universe can exist without me. The link I have with those I am kin to, the link I have with this beautiful autumn dawn is no less than that – it is indeed because of this that the resplendent void gathers my inner soul and merges it into itself in this way. Otherwise could it touch my mind even the tiniest bit? Otherwise could I have felt it as the beautiful? ... The deep-rooted relationship I maintain endlessly with the eternal life of the universe finds its visible and various language in song and colour and fragrance. In every direction the ceaseless expression of this language is continually swaying our minds, consciously and unconsciously; the conversation carries on day and night."

The creative power deep within me that I have written of in this letter, the power that confers unity and significance on all the joy and sorrow and circumstance of my life, is weaving onto one strand the myriad forms of myself and my chain of lives, through which I can feel the unity within the universe. It is this that I addressed as "Jibandebata" and wrote –

Deepest-of-all,
within my soul's depth now you fall,
and have you slaked your thirst?
With a thousand streams of pain and pleasure
I have filled your cup's full measure,
wringing my heart with a pressure cruel —
kneading it to grape-burst!
Scent on scent and hue on hue,
so many songs and rhythms too —
it is your wedding-bed with these
I made, weaving away.
Melting, melting the gold of desire,
I have fashioned from the fire
images that stay ever-new,
for your moment's play.

The surprising thing is this, I am coming to be, I am finding expression. What an endless sweet delight there is in me, which is why I am standing with open eyes amidst this light and this sky, nurtured by all the strength of the countless suns and moons and planets and stars of the limitless universe — I am abandoned by none. But a question springs up in my mind: how am I fortifying the right of this amazing existence of mine? This love for me, this joy that tirelessly carries on, without whose presence I would not have had the power to exist myself — am I contributing nothing to it?

You have welcomed me. What hopes
you had I cannot tell.
Monarch of Life, did you delight
in my dawn and in my night,
in my labour, in my play,
where you lonely dwell?
In winter, autumn, monsoon, spring,
all the songs my soul would sing —

alone upon your throne, did you
      discern that melody?
Was there a garland for your wearing
in the flowers of my mind's bearing?
In the woodland of my youth
      did your heart roam free?

What do you see in my soul, dear friend?
      Do your eyes not harden
at my failings, falterings, flaws —
      or do they grant pardon?
Days and nights of worship bereft,
so often the deity has left,
as flowers-of-offering pine, unplucked
      in a lonely garden.
You tuned a veena *to your way:*
ever more slackly its strings play.
O Poet, the song that you composed,
      how shall I ever sing?
Going to water your flowery glade
I fell asleep under the shade.
In the dusk with brimming tears
      water now I bring.

If it is the case that all the scope that lay in my present life of serving this Jibandebata has been exhausted, if the fuel of my present life is in ashes and cannot be renewed, then will he allow the fire that he wanted to keep burning to be extinguished? How long does it take to dispose of unwanted ashes? Yet why should this flame of light die out on that account? It is very clear that it is not an object of neglect. Deep within one knows there is no end to the unwavering glance of joy upon it.

Is it all at an end, my lord and friend,
      all that there was of mine?

Sleep's blind power, the wakening hour –
that song, life, beauty fine?
Is life's bower to fill with light,
that was the trysting-place of night?
Loosened is the embrace of arms,
my kisses have lost their wine.
Then break up the court of today
and bring new forms, a new array
of beauty. I the ever-old
you take again as new.
Bring me within life's bond, I pray,
that wedding-tie renew.

The advent I have felt in my personal life, that from within the past and from what is to come touches life's sail with the breeze of love, and that carries me to new *ghats* on the great river of time, is the Jibandebata that I spoke of.

At moments of leisure on life's journey, when I have taken the opportunity to look at the world clearly and unwaveringly, another sensation has overwhelmed me. The sense of an unbroken link between me and the natural universe, an ever-old oneness of being, has exerted a deep pull. Sitting on a boat so often I have let go my inner soul for its complete dispersal over the water, land and sky alight with the sun's rays. Then I have no longer kept earth at a distance because it is earth, then water's stream has flowed through my soul in a song of delight. At that very moment I could say –

If I turn into earth, water, grass,
flower or fruit – if it come to pass
I return to Earth in the animal class,
why in the world should I care?
In the limitless bond wherever I pass,
a kinship is ever there.

At that time too I wrote –

> *Take me back, O Earth, and draw*
> *this child of your lap within once more,*
> *beneath your mighty garment's fold.*
> *Mother, mixed in your clay's mould,*
> *I reach out everywhere with the quick joy*
> *of Spring.*

I did not hesitate to say this –

> *Merging me with your clay,*
> *with tireless feet you make your way*
> *now here, now there in the endless sky,*
> *circle the sun as aeons go by*
> *of countless days and nights. Your grass*
> *has risen in me, and a mass*
> *of flowers has bloomed, and in me showers*
> *of pollen-dust, leaves, fruit and flowers*
> *have rained down from great trees.*

I have no pride in separate existence – I do not acknowledge any
severance between me and the world.

> *No longer do I vaunt the human soul,*
> *seeing your cool dark-coloured mother's face;*
> *but to your dust and earth give my heart whole.*

I hope readers will understand from this that I have not divided
up my devotion, keeping my soul, the world of nature and the
lord of the world as it were piecemeal in separate compartments.

Whether through the soul or through the world I find no end
to amazement. I cannot dismiss anything and call it inanimate or
limited. Within what is limited and visible the manifestation of
the endless is a perpetual source of wonder to me. That I am
travelling with open eyes here through water and land, flora and
fauna, moon and sun, day and night, is quite extraordinary. This

universe is astonishing in its molecules and atoms, in its every speck of dust. The fire and the wind, the sun and the moon, the clouds and the lightning our ancestors saw with a lofty supernal vision. That they journeyed life-long through the unimaginable greatness of the world with a living devotion and a sense of wonder – that every touch of the world sounded ever-new thrilling hymn-songs on the *veena* of their soul – this touches my inmost heart. There are those who wish airily to dismiss the sun as a ball of fire, as if they knew what fire was! There are those who conclude that the Earth is a ball of clay, an orb "with water channels ringed"; who think that to call water water, is to comprehend all water, and to call earth earth, is to let it become earth! Regarding Nature I will quote from three old letters of mine.

"Such beautiful days and nights disappear constantly from my life – I cannot absorb them fully. All this colour, this light and shade, this sky-pervading silent array, this all-space-suffusing peace and beauty in the midst of Earth and Heaven – is the arrangement that makes for these a small thing? How immense this festival-ground! Such a large and amazing concern is being carried on outside us every day, and a proper response to it within us alas is not available. We live at such a distance from the universe! The light of one star reaches this Earth across light years, taking thousands of centuries, journeying a path of endless darkness, and it cannot enter our soul! It is as if the mind is many more light years away! The colourful mornings and the colourful evenings are dropping off one by one into the waters of the ocean, like jewels from the torn garlands of the nymphs of the directions, and not even one lands up in our mind!... The Earth we have fallen into, the people here are all strange creatures. Day and night they never stop putting up walls, constructing rules – they hang up curtains, in case they see something with their own two eyes – really Earth's creatures are very strange! It is surprising that they haven't placed an enclosure round every flowering tree, or rigged up an awning against the moon. In self-imposed blindness they are riding through the world in their enclosed palanquins – looking at what?"

"Once when I was one with this Earth and the green grass grew upon me, the light of autumn came down, and in sunlight from every pore of my far-stretching green body the fragrant warmth of youth began to rise, and under the bright sky I would lie silently spanning the land and water of many far-distant countries. At such a moment of autumn sunlight in the huge entirety of my body the essences of joy and the vitalities of life one by one would gather in a half-conscious, utterly inexpressible and immense manner – some of this comes into my mind. The state of mind I am in seems to be the condition of this eternally blossoming and blooming, thrilled, sun-accompanied, primaeval Earth. It seems this current of consciousness is slowly coursing through every blade of grass and every tree's roots and veins, the entire crop-field is falling under a spell, and every coconut-tree leaf is a-quiver with the passion of life."

"This Earth here is eternally new to me like someone I have loved for many days and many lives. ... I can very well remember many aeons ago, this maiden world had just raised her head from a bath in the ocean and was singing a hymn to the young sun of the time – I had flowered as a tree in the first effusion of life from somewhere on Earth's new ground. There were no living creatures on Earth, the huge ocean swayed day and night and like a senseless mother engulfed her tiny newborn land in a frantic embrace from time to time. On this Earth then I drank in the sun's first rays with my whole body – like an infant child I trembled in the blind thrill of life under a blue sky, and embracing this earth-mother of mine with all my roots I drank her breast-milk. In a dumb joy my flowers bloomed and my new leaves came out. When the monsoon clouds thickened, the splendour of their deep darkness would visit my leaves with the familiar touch of the palm of a hand. Then after that I was born in many a new age in the soil of this Earth. Whenever the two of us sit facing each other in solitude, I am reminded a little of this age-old acquaintance of ours. At the moment my Earth is seated on the crop-field, on that river-bank, wearing a scarf of yellow-gold sunlight. I am sprawled near her feet, near her lap. Just as some mothers do not look much at the comings and goings of their children, in a half-conscious but motionless patience, my Earth this afternoon is looking at that horizon and thinking back to early primaeval times – she is not glancing much at me, and I am only babbling ceaselessly."

Nature has enchanted me with her forms and essences of beauty, her colours and fragrances, Mankind with his intelligence and mind, his affection and love – and I do not distrust that enchantment, I do not criticise it. It is not imprisoning me, rather it is liberating me; it has made me reach out beyond myself. Towing the boat does not tie the boat back, it draws it on further ahead. All the world's fetters of attraction help us to move ahead in this way. Someone who is moving fast is aware of his own speed; someone else moving slowly may imagine himself stuck in the same place. But everyone has to move on – in the ceaseless pull of the world's daily affairs, everyone to a greater or lesser extent is being extended away from his own direction and towards the godhead. Whatever we may think, we are not tied down to one place by our brother, our dear one, our son. A lamp's light reveals not only what we are looking for, it lights the whole room. Love expands, transcending the object of love. Through the beauty of the world, through the sweetness of dear ones, God himself is drawing us out – no one else has any power at all to do so. Through love that is of the Earth a joy in the abundance and diversity of Creation is felt; through the beauty of the world a deeper beauty is witnessed: this indeed is what I call the endeavour to find salvation. I am enchanted in the world, and in that enchantment I taste salvation's elixir. –

Renunciation's no escape for me.
Rather as one tied down endlessly
I'll taste salvation's joys. Earth's clay cup
with your nectar ever again fills up,
so scented, hued. My daily world will flame
a thousand lamp-flames all within that same
one flame of yours burning in your temple.
The yogi I'll not take for my example:
to shut the doors of sense is not for me.
Delight of sight, of smell, of melody –
every delight has your delight at heart.
The blind enchantment I take for my part
will light up as salvation. I shall see
my love's fruition, as a devotee.

As a boy I wrote *Prakritir Pratisodh* ("Nature's Revenge"). I don't know that I had a clear understanding of it then, but this theme was in it – that when we accept this world, rely on this worldly home, venerate the world about us, we can realise the Endless in its true meaning. The attempt to jump off the ship in which countless millions have set out on their voyage, and to cross the ocean by swimming, will never be successful.

O world, O great boat, where are you going?
Gather me up into your shelter.
Alone and swimming, I make no headway.
Millions are out upon their voyage –
I too long to be with them there.
Where the sun and the moon shine torches
I shun the path and abandon the light –
but why do I spend my life in darkness,
a tiny glow-worm, seeking a path? . . .
When a bird flies into the sky
it thinks, "I have left the Earth behind –"
it flies and flies, it soars so high –

there is no way it can quit the Earth.
Weary at last it comes to the nest.

When at a mature age I wrote the play *Malini* ("Girl of the Gardens"), I spoke in a similar way about the realisation of religion as evolving from far to near, from the general to the particular, from the imagination to what lies visibly around –

> *I see that religion loves as a mother loves,*
> *is loved as a son is loved; as a donor gives*
> *it gives, and again as one in need receives;*
> *it blesses as a guru, and humbly kneels*
> *as a disciple; a lady-love, it compels*
> *the wellspring of love from a stone soul – and then,*
> *a passionate heart, it gives up all again.*
> *Religion casts a net of the heart upon*
> *the world-abode of people. To love's lap*
> *the universe is drawn and gathered up.*
> *A great bond fills my soul with joy and pain.*

The little I needed to say about myself is almost finished now, and with some final words I shall reach a conclusion –

> *What you gift the Earth's citizens, Lord,*
> *satisfies all hopes yet can afford*
> *a further bounty. When all else has passed,*
> *your whereabouts are sought and found at last.*
> *Each day the river streams, but when its chores*
> *are done, in water-offerings it pours*
> *about your feet in never-ending rill.*
> *The flower's fragrance the whole world may fill,*
> *and does it find fulfilment there? Not quite:*
> *its last awakening is in your rite.*
> *Your rite takes nothing from the world away.*
> *Of all the words a poet speaks in his lay,*

with many minds their many senses gleaning,
it runs to you, the full and final meaning!

I have tried to present the main theme of my poetry and life partly by quotation from poems and partly by explanation. I do not know if I have been able to present it clearly – for the task of its clarification is not entirely in my hands – much depends on the one who is to understand. One suspects many readers will say that the poetry remained a riddle and the life likewise. If the power of the world is uttered in my imagination and life in the form of a message that is unintelligible to others, so that my poetry and life are of no use to anyone in the world – it is my own loss, my own failure. And so there is no point in railing at me, to correct it is impossible for me – I had no other way.

When the universe is expressed in human language, through the human heart and life, then there is little profit if it appears only as echoes and reflections. We obtain but a small fraction of the identity of the world by way of the senses – from age to age through the souls of dreamers, poets and visionary sages we make that acquaintance complete in newer and deeper forms. To take a lyric poet and mark his poems as good or mediocre, breaking them up in a piecemeal examination, is not the true work of a critic. But how the world is expressing itself throughout his entire poetry, the message it takes shape in, is what should claim our understanding. Using the poet as her instrument, in what form does the *veena*-bearing goddess Vani, the world's expressive power, manifest herself? – this is the theme to take a look at.

What is inexpressible in the world, and has struck at the gates of the poet's heart again and again, if that finds speech in the poet's poetry – what in the world is beyond beauty, and comes and gazes every day at the face of the poet, if that beauty beyond form gains form in the poet's poetry – what has taken shape as an image before the eyes, if that pervades itself as a feeling in the poet's poetry – if what wanders homeless in the form of a disembodied feeling, finds a full embodiment in the poet's poetry – then and then only has the poetry succeeded; and that successful poetry itself is the true biography of the poet. To try to capture the subject of that biography in the everyday facts of the poet's life is a travesty.

> *Don't peek and peer from the outside*
> *to outside, so to speak.*
> *Don't seek out my heart's suffering,*
> *from joy and grief I will not spring,*
> *my face won't show you anything,*
> *the poet's not where you seek. ...*
>
> *A figure of dream and secret going,*
> *unknown to himself, to others' knowing –*
> *is it this me, the poet, showing,*
> *outmatched in my song's strife?*
> *– Or the human shape that's shut in the house,*
> *laid low at every moment's force,*
> *a feverish prey to praise, to abuse –*
> *the poet's there, in that life?*

1311*

2

ABOUT SOMETHING THAT COMES at the wrong time the mind is always apprehensive. The appreciation I have received from you is an untimely fruit – so one is afraid that at any moment it may fall from its stalk.

Poets may expect to receive both small payment and salaries for their services to literature, as is the practice with other workers. They are on the lookout for small payments of fame, as if to satisfy a daily hunger – their days cannot be passed in a mere fast. But there are poets who arrange for their own rewards – they supply their remuneration from their own joy, without householders donating even a handful of grain.

So this is their daily pittance – hard-won at the day's end and it ebbs with the day. After that comes the salary. But it cannot be claimed before the month is over. That eternal reward, it is not customary to ask for it during one's lifetime. The calculation of this salary is usually done in Chitragupta's accounts office. Virtually no mistake is ever made there.

But whenever payment is arranged before that, in one's lifetime, it is somewhat suspect. In the world much that is won by fluke can be kept to the end. Many have become rich by cheating others – examples of this are not so uncommon. But fame lacks this advantage. Here the principle of non-expiry does not hold. Confiscation is immediate once the fraud is exposed. This is the law of Time. So there is no scope for feeling confident about the honours a poet receives in his lifetime.

And not only this. If a salary is obtained during one's lifetime the money does not fall entirely into the poet's hands. Someone camps day and night outside the poet's door, extorting a commission. However great a poet he may be, the whole of him is not a poet. The pride that clings to him insists on its share of everything. This presence believes that the credit was all his, and the poetic glory too should fall to his share. And so he keeps packing it all away. This is how the priest steals the sacrament. But after death that pest of a pride-personage ceases to exist, and what is due reaches its proper destination.

The greatest thief in the world is the ego. He does not feel embarrassed to claim even what belongs to God Himself. This is why there are many elaborate procedures to suppress the rogue, keep him under. This is why Manu said: "Know that honour is as poison, insult is as nectar." Wherever honour entices, it is better to shun all contact, as far as possible.

I have reached the age of fifty. Now the call of the forest has come. Now is the time for renunciation. Now it will not do to take onto one's head the new burden of one's accumulated possessions. So if God rewards me with honour even after the age of fifty, I must understand, it is only to give me a lesson in renunciation. I cannot accept such honour simply as my own. I must set down the head-burden in the place where my head is to bow. So I can give you all only this much assurance, that I will not insult the honour you have given me, by using it as material for my ego.

In our country at the present time one may well rejoice at reaching fifty – for long life is rare. A country where people die young is deprived of the riches of experience of old age. Youth is a horse and maturity a charioteer. At times we have undergone the danger of driving the country's chariot without a charioteer for the horses. So in a land where people are short-lived the person who has reached fifty may be cheered on his way.

But the poet is neither scientist nor philosopher nor historian nor politician. Poetry is the dawn-of-grace of man's first expression. When the expanse of life before one has not yet discovered its boundaries, when hope is full of pure mystery – only then does poetry's song rise in notes ever-new. Still the beauty of the mystery is by no means of dawn alone; even at the dusk of life's completion the radiant hints of the pure mystery of eternal life announce its deeper beauty. But the quiet solemnity of that mystery silences the exuberance of song. So I ask, what is a poet's age worth?

The appreciation I receive, then, at the beginning of old age may not be regarded as a fitting tribute to maturity. Even at this age you have given me a young man's due. Indeed it is a poet's true tribute. It is not respect, nor devotion, it is the heart's affection. We offer someone our devotion according to the measure of his greatness, our respect according to the measure of his competence; but affection uses no rule of measurement. When love begins its homage it gives itself entire.

It is not due to intellectual strength, nor to a weight of learning, nor to piety's excellence, but if after years of flute-playing I have won your heart with one of my tunes – then I am deeply enriched, and at once accept that love. For just as in love's giving itself no reckoning is made, so the one who is fortunate enough to receive it need fear no reckoning of his worth. The person who can offer the gift of love is truly powerful – the one who receives it, merely fortunate.

Today especially I can feel how great the power of love is. What I have received is nothing trivial. The salary we pay a servant is a trifle, and the great value we set on adulation is a demeaning thing. I have not prayed for that contemptible gift, neither have you given it. It is a gift of love that I have received. This love has a noble essence. We can't accept any defect in an article we pay for – if there's a hole or stain anywhere we demand a refund. When we pay labour charges we levy a fine for defective workmanship. But love can bear much, can pardon much; in accepting injury it expresses its own greatness.

I have devoted myself to the pursuit of literature for over forty years now, and without doubt have made many blunders and given offence again and again. This garland you have honoured me with, overlooking all my incompletenesses, all my wounding words and diatribes, can be nothing other than a garland of love. In this offering is your true glory, and it glorifies me as well.

Where the law of natural selection is strong, there is bound to be a natural abundance. Where much is born much dies – only a little lasts. Poets who are highly skilled in a mechanical way, "artists", create under the guidance of a cerebral selection, and do not allow natural selection a look-in. Whatever they give expression to becomes only too meaningful.

I know that there is a huge abundance in my work that suffers failure to a marked degree. There is little room in the boat of immortality, so the more I can cut down my luggage, the more chance I have of crossing over the river of extinction. It is not true that the more we hand over to Eternity, the more she will accept. My luggage has become only too heavy – and that is indication enough that the larger part of it is already stamped for death. The charioteer of immortality adorns himself with golden crown, diamond chains and jewelled armour; he doesn't carry a sack on his head.

But I have been unable to create the simply-turned yet precious ornaments of a master craftsman. I have packed my luggage with whatever has come my way; its weight is greater than its worth. Just as wastage is a fact of life so too much hoarding is a nuisance. I have been prone to this folly in literature. The Customs Office where all goods are checked will not pass all that I have deposited. But I don't want to complain of the fear of loss. On the one hand there is Eternity, on the other there is the instant. Whatever I have supplied to the need of the moment, to its celebration, even to its unnecessary dissipation, has little durability but it cannot be said to be entirely fruitless on that account. I see at least one result: that by abundance alone my poetic endeavours have occupied the heart of the present time to a degree, and I have no doubt that the affection I have received today from my readers is to a large extent in return for this abundance.

But just as my gifts are ephemeral so the return is not everlasting. Of the flowers I have made blossom a great number will fall, and so the garlands you have given me will mostly wither. What a poet receives in his lifetime is actually a settling of dues with the present moment. I should not allow myself to forget that today's special occasion of necessity includes my squaring of accounts with the moment.

Many omissions, intentional or unintentional, are possible in these transactions with the present moment. We can load ourselves with a great burden of failure, we can talk more than we can think, more attention is claimed by custom than by worth, imitation surpasses true feeling. I must admit that in my long career in literature all these lapses, with or without my knowledge, have occurred and accumulated.

I should say only one thing on my own behalf, and that is that to this day I have offered to literature only such pieces as I thought to be worthy of it. I have not tried to cater to popular demand. Instead of fitting my work to the demands of popular taste I have shaped it to my own taste and set it in the court of literature. That is to pay that court its real tribute. And whatever such an approach may bring, to be sure it does not bring unremitting applause, and my case is no exception. The touch that sweetens the fare of my fame, late on in my life, is a new experience for me. The form and the diction I used when I started writing poetry were not appreciated in their time and I cannot say they deserve appreciation even now. I have only this to say: I gave to others what was mine alone. I did not adopt an easier expedient. Often you may please only by deception – but that very pleasing will deceive you in its turn, after a time. To that cheap pleasure I have never bent a greedy eye.

Aside from this I have frequently made unpalatable remarks in my work, and at once I have had to endure the consequences of such offence. One can achieve one's own real development by one's own strength, permanent benefit never comes through begging and petition – I have not been able to utter this old platitude without facing the bitterest abuse. Such things have happened again and again. But I have never courted popularity by selling off in the market-place what I know to be true. I respect my country with all my heart; I have nowhere seen anything to compare with what is finest in my people. For this reason whenever the dust and garbage of difficult times have at all obscured the treasure of our constant striving, I have not expressed any pity at all for the state of affairs – and it is in this that I have sharply differed from my readers and my audience, time and time again. I know this disagreement is very strong and its impact is terrible: in such discord we imagine a friend an enemy, we name a blood relation a stranger. But I have myself endured the impact of giving such offence. I have not tried to be tactful and avoid unpleasantness.

That is why I humbly acknowledge the very exceptional appreciation I have received from you today. This is no cheap flattery, it is a gift of love. It honours not only the recipient but the giver too. The society in which a person can be honoured without compromising his true ideals or falsifying his true opinion is in the proper sense a society that commands respect. Where people are forced to market their truth in order to gain admiration, admiration itself is not admirable. Where praise and honour are distributed according to whether one is of one's own party or not, honour itself is contemptible. If people throw dust on you in disgust, in such a world the dust itself is your true adornment. If they hurl abuse in anger, then that abuse is your real applause.

Where honour is great, where it is true, the mind of itself bows meekly down. So before I take my leave of you today I can tell you that I clasp your gift of honour to my head and treasure it as my country's blessing. It is something sacred, not an object for my own gratification. It will purify my soul, not excite my self-pride.

Phalgun 1318

(Mid-February to mid-March 1912)

3

EVERYONE HAS SOMETHING special called "my religion". But he has no clear knowledge of it. He knows, "I am a Christian, I am a Muslim, a Vaishnavite, a Shakta," and so on. But even if he is certain from birth till death that he belongs to an established religion, he may be mistaken. The very assumption of a name erects such a screen that the inner religion itself escapes his notice.

Which is his religion? The one that lies hidden in his heart and keeps on creating him. An inherent religion and instinct of life builds up all that is animal and living. The animal need not have any sense of that religion. Man has another being, greater than his physical being – it is his humanity. The creativity that is inside this being is his religion. For this reason *dharma* (religion) is a very significant word in our language. The wateriness of water is the religion of water, the fieriness of fire the religion of fire. Similarly man's religion is his innermost truth.

In every man truth has a universal form and at the same time an individual form. That is his personal religion. And in that he is preserving the variety of the world. This variety is an invaluable element of creation. And so we do not have the power to destroy it completely. However much I may follow the rule of "sameness", I can by no means blot out the difference between my form and the form of others. Similarly however much I may think that by assuming a communal label I have come to belong to the common religion of my group, still my own religious soul knows that a certain individuality of my personal religion exists at the root of my humanity. That individuality is the special joy of the soul that sees without and within.

But as I said earlier, what is apparent from outside is my non-individual religion. That common identity is my religious identity in society. It is like a turban on my head. But the brain that is in my head, that is invisible, the identity that is manifest to my religious soul – if suddenly someone from outside were to say it had leaked out through the surrounding shell of its vital mystery, and if further he analysed its components and proceeded to confine it to a certain category – one would be left astonished.

That is how it is with me. A recently-published article has come out with the news that I have a religious creed and it is of a certain class and kind.

If someone were to tell me that he saw my ghost I would be no less concerned. For one's ghostly life doesn't begin till the worldly one is over. To say my ghost has appeared is as good as saying that my present life has ceased to be real for me, and my past is all the reality that remains. My religion exists at the very root of my life. This life continues; but the news that at some point its religion has come to a halt, so that it can be displayed before curious visitors in a museum for the price of a ticket, is hard to believe.

A few years ago another writer in another newspaper published a review of my religious songs. In it he deliberately cited a few of my adolescent compositions to build up towards his own desired conclusion. To take a photograph that suggests I have come to a halt when I have not done so, is to embarrass me. The picture of a running horse with its legs kicking high does not prove that its legs were always up in the air and are up in the air now. That is why a movement looks comic in a photograph, only an artist's brush can capture its essence.

Perhaps this does not convey the whole of it. Maybe an edge of what is rooted in the unexplored depths of consciousness has leapt to view. And the moment of its emergence marks the start of its interaction with the external world. Whenever that interaction begins the world sticks its convenient classifying label on it and feels relieved. For otherwise it is impossible to fix its price or use.

A person's reputation is based on the way he is known to the outside world. If this external identity does not agree in any way with his inner truth then a split enters his existence. Because a person is not only what he is inside himself, he exists largely in the way he is known to all. "Know thyself" is not the final truth; "let thyself be known" is also of great importance. The attempt to let oneself be known is everywhere in the world. So it is that my inner religion fails to lock itself up within itself – it must necessarily go on making itself known to the outside in various ways that are both apparent and still not apparent to me.

There is no end to this process of making oneself known. If there is any truth in it then it continues even after death. So one may ask what exactly is lost if this self-revelation should cease. A poet simply has to bear without complaint whatever is said about his poetry. For it's a matter of taste. A matter of taste cannot be settled by argument. It is settled by time. Time's patience is infinite, and taste must follow it; it cannot hope to obtain all its dues at once. But if there is anything called "my religion" it would be an injustice to myself and to others not to have cleared away a wrong impression about it. So if a solicitous critic says something that to my mind is an inaccurate representation of the essence of my interaction with others, the use and worth of which really ought to be properly ascertained, it would be impertinent to keep quiet about it.

But it must be admitted that my utterances on religion are like the travelling-notes of a wayfarer. The words of those who have spoken after reaching their destination are sure and certain. They can see their words in a detached way, as clear and apart from themselves. I have never looked at my creed with such detachment. Its complete picture may be drawn by all the marks it has left behind in my various works, in the process of its becoming and growing. The problem in this is that how one arranges these ingredients with the right pieces from head to tail to form a whole, depends largely on one's personal predilections. Whatever others may do with them, I want to piece together these ingredients for myself in order to see the picture that emerges.

I HAVE HEARD it said that my religion is under a flute-song's enchantment, that it leans more towards the tranquil than to the strong and virile. It is essential that I consider this observation with some care, if only for my own sake.

For some, religion is a genteel means of retreat from the battlefield of life – to find in passivity a kind of holiday in which there is no embarrassment, in which there is even some glory. That is to say, to banish from life and existence such episodes as would exempt one from the burden of duty, to turn away from all this in the name of religion and to heave a sigh of relief – is what some see as the purpose of religion. Such people are called *bairagis* (renunciants). On the other hand there are the *bhogis* (hedonists) who lace spirituality with a few special worldly sensations and drink of it to forget the rest of the world. Which is to say that one yearns for a peace that excludes the world, while the other longs for a heaven in which the world is forgotten. Both of them look at the path of escape as the path of religion.

Yet there are those who discover religion in the fulfilment of a vision of reality in which the world is seen in all its pain and pleasure, struggles and conflicts. The world seen merely as the world does not reveal that supreme meaning which runs through and across it as warp and weft together, outgrowing it on all sides. That is why they view religion not as truth with some of its aspects overlooked, but as the apprehension of the supreme meaning of reality in all its completeness.

Truancy from school may have two ends: one, to do no work, and two, to follow one's inclination in play. There is a pain in the rigour of school that one scales a wall or bribes a gatekeeper to escape. But again there are two sides to enduring the pain of hard work. Some boys submit to discipline from fear of punishment, while others simply find refuge in the habitual discipline – feeling secure in their mechanical obedience to authority day in day out in the correct manner, at the fit time. And they feel a satisfaction as if in something gained. But boys of these two types look at discipline as something absolute, and see nothing beyond it.

But there is also a kind of schoolboy who embraces the pain and rigour of work, voluntarily and even with delight, because he has truly recognised the purpose of school. It is through this understanding that he is able to conquer the pain as soon as he meets it, to liberate his mind from the chain of discipline as soon as he accepts it. This is a true emancipation. To find freedom in the avoidance of rigour is actually self-deception. It is because he can see before him a radiant picture of the fullness of knowledge that this boy knows all the incompleteness, all the pain, all the restraints of the present moment as elements of that great joy. It is quite impossible for this boy to play truant. The delight he finds in embracing the pain is greater than the pleasure of no work and all play. This delight is more precious than peace, more beautiful than the flute's song.

Now the question is, which religion is it that I recognise as my own? One thing must be kept in mind, that when I say "my religion" it is not to suggest that I have attained fulfilment in a particular belief. To say "I am a Christian" is not to suggest that one is like Christ – numerous transgressions of Christianity may show in daily conduct. To say that I never violate my religion either in speech or action would be a falsehood I would not wish to indulge in. Still the question remains, what are the ideals of my religion?

The answer to this is of course scattered over my writings. When I put this question to my inner self I meet with the reply – I cannot part with even a fraction, since every part seems to make me whole.

I want to take in all, with all outside —
my brothers! — so to mix and be allied.

When I see truth with any part lacking then I deny the very truth of it. The mark of truth is that it is all-embracing. Whatever inconsistencies may temporarily appear in its make-up, there is a profound consistency at its core, for otherwise it would have destroyed itself. Consistency is a property of truth; therefore to produce a home-made consistency by patchwork and omission is to obstruct truth itself. There was a time when Man idly conceived the Earth as a lotus-flower with Mount Sumeru at the centre like a seed-case, and the continents spreading out like petals in every direction. At the root of this conception is the belief that truth has a harmony, without which it cannot hold and keep itself together.

This belief is justified. But the harmony is not without contradiction — it is something that embraces disharmony and is greater than all discord — just as Shiva was able to drink all the poison of the sea's churning and so be the more himself. In the same way if one respects truth one ought to have the courage to know the world as it materially is — divided into many uneven fragments. I have no desire for tailored truth and home-made consistency. I desire far more and am not at all afraid of inconsistency.

When I was young, for various reasons I had little contact with humanity; it was with Nature that in my privacy I had a real bond. This bond is essentially a harmonious one, because in it there is neither struggle nor conflict, no mind pitted against mind, will against will. This condition is indeed the true condition of childhood. Peace and sweetness are most needed in the privacy of the home at this time. The seed needs to absorb the sap in peace as it rests in the heart of the ground below the screen of the wide Earth. The blow and counterblow of rain and storm and sun and shadow are not for the seed now. In the same way, in a state of shelter under Nature's wings, glimmerings of religious instinct are received in a sense of immensity. Here the child sees the One who is all Peace (*shantam*), and grows up in the shadow of the One who is all Truth (*satyam*).

It is easy to feel this communion of one's own nature with Nature, because there is no interference of other souls with one's own. Yet in this very communion we do not ever find complete satisfaction. Because we have a soul and that seeks a greater communion. It is possible to have this wider union not with Nature, but only with humanity. We seek union with our greater ego by spreading ourselves over this wider field. There we seek our great father, friend, lord, the leader of our work, the guide on our path. There when I go about with only my minor ego, my human state is distressed: death haunts me, loss saddens me, the present devastates the future, grief and sorrow turn out to be only too extreme for me to find consolation elsewhere. Then I stake my life on hoarding what comes my way, I find no sense in surrendering anything, a petty envy and malice prey upon the mind – and then –

> *the stain of merely passing through life's day,*
> *the burden of shame,*
> *as night after night a closed room is smoke-blackened*
> *in a lamp's small flame.*

When this yearning to seek the greater self began to flower in my poetry, that is when the seed pierced the earth as a shoot and appeared in the open, it made itself known in "Vishwanritya" ("Cosmic Dance") in *Sonar Tari* ("The Golden Boat") –

> *In tone so vast and deep and sweet,*
> *who will play this tune?*
> *The mind will soar and dance along,*
> *itself forgetting soon.*
> *The bars will break, great joy will be,*
> *a new beat, a new melody,*

> *a tide will quicken in the heart's sea,*
> *under a full moon.*

But even here is the tunefulness of the instrument. Though the tune is deep indeed, still it is sweet in its depth. Nevertheless the tendency of my poetry is from Nature towards the domain of man. It is striking up an acquaintance with the conscious soul of the universe. In that same poem –

> *Who is it forever playing*
> *in the heart's deep plot*
> *rich tunes on Time's instrument? –*
> *some hear them, some do not.*
> *To their meaning I am blind –*
> *sages seek it, do not find.*
> *The tides of the great human mind*
> *are as the songs allot.*

Here is a reference to the sentient and discerning being who drives the history of universal man through every obstacle and impediment on a path of perilous ups and downs. From now on the period of uninterrupted peace is at an end.

But the unity man is in quest of in conflict and revolution, what is it? It is "the Perfect and the Good" (*shivam*). Within this very excellence lies a considerable contradiction. Here a seedling is about to divide and grow into joy and sorrow, good and evil. What was under the ground, "the Peaceful" (*shantam*), was undivided – there was no conflict there of light and darkness. If the Perfect and the Good is not understood where the conflict breaks out, truth there will pass unrecognised. The pain of knowing this perfection is most severe. Here "great fear is poised like thunder to strike", *mahadbhayam vajramudyatam*. But within this great pain is the real birth of our religious feeling. In the profound peace of Cosmic Nature is its gestation. I have said this about myself in two poems of *Naibedya* ("Offerings").

1

The milk a mother lets flow as she suckles
a joyful lazy child takes in and chuckles.
Such a flood of feelings as a boy
at Nature's breast I drank in with great joy,
and on its wild fifth note the flute I played.
My soul that in a child's delight was laid,
so gently reared, received from dusk and dawn
and night, as if in cup on cup bride-borne,
honey of all hues, in with the scent of flowers.
Today if that trance, that sweet spell of hours
is ended, if the magic to be met
at Nature's touch is gone — there's no regret.
You led me out, away from that child's bliss,
from village up to grand metropolis.
Only allow my soul strength to endure,
and show me truth, in its hard form and pure.

2

I stand amid the heat of battle's blows.
Bracelets, bangles, necklaces — all those
I have flung far away. With your own hand
select for me your arrows where I stand —
all-accurate, from a fund that's never spent.
Initiate me in your armament,
Master of War. Your love, so fatherly
and powerful, let it cry out to me
its hard command. In new heroic armour
let me assume the burden and the honour
of a grave duty, harshest pain to bear.
The ornaments of wounds shall be my wear.
In each of his attempts your servant bless,

in his success and in his unsuccess.
Let him not sink down in sweet feeling's sea,
but labour well and independently.

The longing to have one's desires fulfilled, through reliance on the good that gives the human soul courage and leads it through pain and conflict, has found utterance in the poem "Ebar Phirao More" ("Now Call Me Back") in *Chitra* ("The Colourful Enchantress"). The poem begins with a reproving word about the flute's song –

The day I came to this Earth, here to be,
who was the mother whose sole gift to me
was but this flute to play? By my own song
enchanted, as I played, beyond the long
days and nights I went, past the world's bounds.

The tranquillity that belongs to sweetness is not this poem's aim. With whom is the tryst in the poem?

Who is it? One I do not know or mark –
but this alone I know – that in night's dark,
blasted by the storm, the thunder's rage,
it is for that One that from age to age,
shielding the soul's lit lamp, he goes along,
the human traveller. Who has heard the song
of that One – all I know is this – the world
he gives up, into danger's whirlpool hurled;
he bares his breast for torture, hears the roar
of death as if it were a song, no more.
Burned by the fire, by the axe split apart,
pierced by the pike, still all calm at heart,
whatever's dear to him, he gives the same
as fuel to the sacrificial flame
life-long. At last he gives a heart that's torn,
a blood-red lotus, in the last rite borne

flamewards, a devoted offering.
So life is at a final reckoning,
fulfilling in its death the living soul.

After this the great soul and the individual soul at blow and counterblow began at times to appear in my poetry. The interplay of the two is not always a thing of sweetness or comfort. The call that comes from the infinite is after all not the mellifluous tune of the flute. I have answered it in this way –

Now cruel one, now enchantress,   now bloodthirsty mistress
                    of dour might,
I have given you my day,   and will you snatch away,
                    at the end, my night?
To all that live, nearby   the mortal limits lie,
                    an end's at hand;
then why, heart-rending, fierce,   do you each ending pierce
                    with your command?
In a world imbued   with darkness, solitude
                    attends on all.
Deep within it, where,   like thunder on the air,
                    is your great call?

This call is certainly a call to strength: a summons to the field of action – not to a pleasant bower of sensations. And so my final reply is –

Victory will be, will be,   goddess, a brave victory,
                    it will be mine.
I shall fulfil it all,   all the utterance of your call,
                    great queen, divine.
The tired hand will not quiver,   nor will the voice shiver,
                    the veena *not break –*
my lamp will burn all night –   for the new morning's light
                    I'll keep awake.

In the new dawn I'll give   duty's prerogative
          to the new servant's hand —
still in my last word   as I go, shall be heard
          your call and command.

Here are distinct and indistinct footprints of the gradual passage
of my faith from within the darkness of my subconscious world
towards the light of the conscious. Judging by the trail it is clear
that the traveller neither knows the path nor is he aware of the
direction. Nor has he understood whether the path leads to the
familiar world or beyond it. What he can see he cannot give a
name to, and he tries various names. He was picking his way
towards the destination he had in mind, when suddenly he was
surprised to find that someone had been leading him in a different
direction.

> *But you confuse all my steps so,*
> *the way for sure I cannot know.*
> *Bewildered, weary as I go,*
> *   a strange land here I see.*
> *Now I tread a hill-top high,*
> *now in pain's dark cave I lie ...*
> *as like a madman I go by*
> *   a way not known to me.*

Before the poet who took this twilit road there glimmered
now and then a certain revelation. This experience found expression in a letter of the time; allow me to quote a couple of
passages from it —

"Who is solemnly and sonorously asking me to look at everything, who is compelling me to listen with a calm and attentive
ear to all the songs that are not of this world, who is making the
fine and tough web of my contact with the world every day
keener and more responsive? ...

The religion we acquire from popular scripture never really becomes one's own religion. It is only a bond of habit that links us with it. To awaken religion in oneself is Man's eternal quest. It is to be brought to life through extreme pain. I want to animate it with the blood of my veins, then whether I obtain happiness in life or not, I can die fulfilled in joy."

In this way gradually a condition for the clear acknowledgement of religion within life came into being. As it continued to make headway a break began to appear between my earlier life and the phase to come. Who was it that emerged in the conflict-torn world of Man, terrible and tumultuous, at once tearing apart Nature's pall of sweetness and tranquillity spread over the endless sky? From now on it was to be the sorrow of conflict, the upheaval of revolution. The poem "Varshashesh" ("Year's End") written about this time gives an idea of the advent of this new phase as it appeared with the fury of a tempest –

> *Indomitable, inexorable, merciless, new,*
> > *strong in your ease,*
> *just as fruit scattering dead flowers all around*
> > *its own way frees,*
> *and ripping away the old leaves, finds its form*
> > *all beautiful-new –*
> *so in your great and full power you appear.*
> > *I bow to you.*
> *Dark, tireless, terrible, loving, ever-vivid –*
> > *to you I bow.*
> *Great hero new-born, what you bring with you*
> > *you do not know.*
> *Your flying banner is the burning sunbeam*
> > *through clouds descending.*
> *I glance up, suppliant, at its words, but gain*
> > *no understanding.*

Prince, smiling, draw your bow, and let it twang
*   with its charged sound –*
may the breast's ribs be pierced – that resonance
*   within be found.*
O youth, take up your noble victory-trumpet,
*   issue your call –*
we will stand up, and rush outside, and offer
*   life and all.*
We will not look back, we will not wear fetters and weep,
*   not count the hours,*
not glance aside, not quibble of this and that –
*   free travellers!*

At the first diffusion of the dawn, at the edge of night, its early glow seems no more than decoration. Various colours begin to emerge at the corners of the sky and on the cloud-layers, the tree-tops glimmer, the dew on the grass begins to shimmer, the whole affair seems in the main ornamental. But at least it is clear from all this that the day's act has begun and the night's act is over. It indicates that the sun's touch is felt at the very heart of the sky; it announces that the profound, pervasive, intimate peace of the somnolent night is at an end, and all the strain and effort of waking will in a moment rise to the seventh note, and be reined in by link-notes to break out in the twang of a restless tune. In this way the first appearance of religious feeling was finding tongue in the metaphors of my writing, and with various shades was colouring the clouds of imagination at the peaks of my mental universe. But from within it came the message that the unbroken peace of cosmic Nature was no more, that the term of retreat in solitude in forest and mountain was over, that the first chapter on the battlefield of humanity at large was under way. If we refer to my essay "Pagal" ("The Mad Spirit") that came out about that time in *Bangadarshan* we shall see what exactly sought its utterance through the rhetoric of the imagination. –

"I know that happiness is an everyday term, joy is something beyond that. Happiness shrinks at the slightest possibility of being touched by dust, joy rolls in the dust and shatters the walls of its separation from the cosmos. So for happiness dust is despicable, while for joy it is an adornment. Happiness is afraid lest it lose something. Joy is satisfied to distribute whatever it possesses. That is why for happiness to have nothing is to be poor, while for joy to be poor is to be rich. Happiness cautiously guards its petty ease within the limits of a system. Joy loudly proclaims its beauty within the freedom of destruction and upheaval. So it is that happiness is restricted by rules outside itself, while joy throws off restraint to create its own rules. Happiness waits expectantly for a little nectar. Joy digests without effort things of sorrow. So the inclination of happiness is merely towards the pleasant, while for joy the pleasant and the unpleasant are one and the same.

"There is a mad spirit within Creation: whatever is unthinkable or unexpected he ushers in without rhyme or reason. ... The god of restraining laws is trying to convert the paths of all worldly motions into circles, and this mad spirit is busy leading them astray to make spirals. This mad one in his caprice has evolved birds in the family of reptiles and man in the family of apes. There is a strenuous effort in the world at large to maintain what has been and what is; this mad one is upsetting this order and paving the way for what is not. He has no flute in his hand, the song of harmony is not his, the horn blares out, the rituals set by tradition wither away, and from nowhere an unprecedented state comes and takes its place. ...

"In the monotonous triviality of our everyday life, suddenly the terrible breaks in, its wealth of flaming locks flying. This terrible one awakens as a sudden upheaval in Nature and a tremendous vice in Man. At that awakening how many happy unions have their binding torn apart, how many relationships of the heart are overturned! O Terrible One, the throbbing flame on your brow, that lights a lamp in dark homes with its spark, is the same flame at whose conflagration houses burn in the night amid the cries and wails of a thousand human beings. O Shambhu, at your dance, at your dance-steps to the right and left, great good and great evil erupt in the cosmos. A pall of mere commonness comes to hang over the world at the touch of everyday existence, and you go on tearing it and ripping it with the powerful blows of good and evil. You make the current of life throb on and on with the excitement of the unexpected, only to give expression to power in its newer and newer dance and play, and to creation in its newer and newer forms. Mad spirit, let not my timid heart shrink from taking part in your terrible jubilation. At the centre of the blood-red sky of destruction, may your third eye that is radiant as the rays of the sun illumine my heart of hearts with eternal brilliance. Dance, O mad one, dance. When luminous nebulae spanning millions and billions of miles of sky break into motion at the whirl of this dance, let not the terrible music lose its rhythm in the convulsions of fear in my heart. O conqueror of death, in all our good and evil may victory be yours.

"This whimsical god of ours – I do not mean to suggest he appears only now and again. In truth his madness is ever-present in Creation – we only catch a glimpse of it every now and then. Every day life is renewed by death, good is brightened by evil, the trivial is made precious by the unexpected. When we catch a glimpse, we witness within beauty the rising of something beyond beauty, and the awakening of freedom within bondage."

Thereafter this conviction appeared in my writing again and again – that it is in the form of sorrow and despair, conflict and death that the infinite makes its appearance in life –

> *Is this consummation's way,*
> *   dear one, death of mine?*
> *No auspicious customs, say,*
> *   splendid trappings fine?*
> *Your tawny matted locks awry,*
> *   won't they know a proud tying?*
> *Won't the flag be hoisted high*

of victory, all sides flying?
Won't the river-bank's red eye
   open to your torch-shine?
Won't the ground shake all around,
   dear one, death of mine?

When Shiva sets out to his wedding,
   dear one, death of mine,
details under every heading
   state a great design.
His bull is roaring all around,
   his tiger-hide is flapping,
snakes about his locks are wound
   hissing, rearing, snapping.
To a slapping sound his cheeks rebound,
   while from his neck-line
a string-of-skulls bobs, as his flute sobs,
   dear one, death of mine. ...

If for the house my duties be,
   dear one, death of mine,
shatter the work, embolden me
   such labour to resign.
If all my dreams come true and I
   lie in my bed's keeping,
if swathed in languor's sheets I lie
   half-awake, half-sleeping,
then fill the conch with Ruin's sigh —
   I'll speed, at that sign,
fast and faster, lord and master,
   dear one, death of mine.

Who is the King who makes an appearance in my poem "Agaman" ("Arrival") in *Kheya* ("The Ferry")? He is the Unpeaceful One. Everyone was sleeping peacefully with the door shut at night, without the faintest idea that he would come. Even though there were repeated knocks at the door, and the rumble of his chariot-wheels was heard in dream like the roaring of clouds every now and then, still no one wanted to believe that he was coming, lest it disturb their rest. But the door was thrown open – the King had come.

> *Let the conch-shell be blown,*
> * the door open stand.*
> *The king of the dark chamber*
> * comes at night to command.*
> *Thunder is crashing,*
> *lightning is flashing,*
> *lay out the tattered quilt,*
> * let your yard look grand.*
> *The king of sorrow's night*
> * with the storm is at hand.*

In *Kheya* there is a poem called "Dan" ("The Gift"). The theme is that I wanted a garland of flowers, but what did I receive?

> *No garland is this,*
> * it is your sword.*
> *Fire-flashing, and heavy*
> * as thunder's word –*
> *it is your sword.*

Is it possible to have peace with such a gift? If it is not won through grief and disturbance, peace is a mere bondage.

> *From today within this world*
> * I shall shed my fear.*

Now in everything I do
your glory will appear —
for I shall shed all fear.
Death, where in my room you leave him,
I shall welcome, and receive him
with my whole heart, and believe him
friend and soulmate dear.
Your sword will sever all my chains
and leave me free and clear.
For I shall shed all fear.

Many such songs may be quoted in which the tune is struck of vastness and its discord. But at the same time it must be admitted that this belongs to an intermediate stage, not to the end. The true end is *shantam shivam advaitam*, "the Peaceful One, the Good and the Unique". If terribleness were the ultimate quality of the Terrible, then our souls would not have found refuge in such an incompleteness, and where would the world have gained its preservation? So it is that mankind calls out to him, *Rudra yatte dakshinam mukham tena mam pahi nityam*: O Rudra, with this your gracious face always protect me. That gracious face is the ultimate and the absolute truth. It is a truth that is greater than all that is terrible. But to arrive at it one must needs encounter the terrible. The grace that excludes the terrible, the tranquillity that denies disturbance a place, that is mere dreaming, that is not truth.

Thunder plays about your flute-song.
No light pastoral
sweet notes awaken: but to this
O make me sensible.
Ease will not divert again:
in my heart now I shall gain
pure inspiration from the Life
death makes invisible.

May the storm touch my mind with joy
upon its veena-*strings*
of the seven seas that ten ways dance
while your loud music sings.
Now tear me from my comfort, take me
to those depths, O dear one: make me
know where in the restless surge
peace lies all-powerful.

When I look closely at all my plays, right from *Saradotsav* ("Autumn Festival") up to *Phalguni* ("Song of Spring"), in each of them I hear the same refrain. The king goes out with everyone else to celebrate the autumn festival. He is looking for his companions. On the way he sees some boys who have come out to take part in Nature's autumn carnival. But there is one boy, Upananda, who has abandoned all play to work quietly in a corner in order to pay off his master's bills. The king says he has found his real companion because that boy knows the true joy of communion with Nature in autumn. By the pains he endures he is paying back what is owed to joy – the quality of this suffering is the sweetest. The cosmos too is engaged in this penance of pain: by undergoing a tireless striving it is paying off what it owes to the infinite, having received its gift within itself. By untiring effort every blade of grass expresses its existence, so repaying what is owed to its own inherent reality. In this surrender to relentless pain lies its grace, and here is its festival. By all this it has given Nature at autumn its beauty, and endowed it with joy. Seen from outside it looks like play, yet it is no play, and suffers not the least interruption. Where there is some slackness in repaying the debt to the inherent truth, expression is hampered, ugliness shows, joy is absent. The expression of the soul is full of joy (*ananda*). It is because of this that it can admit of grief and death. The person who avoids this path of sorrow and pain from fear or laziness or uncertainty is denied this bliss in the world. This is the inner statement of *Saradotsav* – it is no tale of sitting beneath a tree listening to the song of a flute.

In the play *Raja* ("King of the Dark Chamber") Sudarshana wished to see her hidden king. Overwhelmed with her own admiration of beauty she placed a garland round the neck of the wrong king; and through that sin and error, she let loose a conflagration and a terrible struggle, and stirred up a tempest inside and outside that drove her to the true union. The path of Creation lies through devastation. So it has been said in the Upanishads, that warmed by the heat He created all this. In our soul's creative process there is pain at every step. But if I see it as pain alone I don't have the complete picture, because in that very pain is beauty and joy.

The consciousness that makes our soul know itself arises through obstacles, pulling down the walls of our habits and comfort. The consciousness that liberates us – *durgam pathastat kavayo vadanti*, "it is a perilous path, so say the seers" – comes beating its victory-drum up the dangerous way of suffering. It makes the horizons shake with terror, so that we see it as our enemy, and after a battle we give it recognition – for "the soul is not attained by the weak", *nayamatma balahinena labhyah*. This idea is discussed in *Achalayatan* ("The Immovable") –

MAHAPANCHAK: Are you our guru?

GRANDFATHER: Yes. You don't know me but I am indeed your guru.

MAHAPANCHAK: You are our guru? Which path have you come by, breaking all our conventions? Who will obey you?

GRANDFATHER: I know I will not be obeyed, but still I am your guru.

MAHAPANCHAK: You are a guru? Then why are you in enemy clothing?

GRANDFATHER: This is my guru's clothing. You will do battle with me – that battle will be my welcome as guru.

MAHAPANCHAK: I will not bow down to you.

GRANDFATHER: I am not going to receive your bow – I will make you bow.

MAHAPANCHAK: Haven't you come to receive our worship?

GRANDFATHER: No, I haven't come to receive your worship, I have come to receive your humiliation.

To my mind the war that rages in Europe today is because that guru has come. He has to pull down the age-old walls of money, of glory, of pride. No one was prepared for his coming. But he was to come with a pageant that had been long in the making. It was because Europe's Sudarshana, enchanted by the beauty of the false king Subarna, mistook him for her husband that the fire burst out, and seven kings found themselves locked in struggle, and the queen must leave her chariot, abandon her wealth, and cross the dust down the path of union to keep her assignation. The idea is in a piece from *Gitali* ("Songs") –

> *A dagger, a necklace*
> *are his, and no more.*
> *He breaks down your door.*
> *He seeks no succour*
> *of alms – but to conquer*
> *your heart by a war.*
> *He breaks down your door.*
> *Up the road of death*
> *to life's very hub*
> *he comes, in war's garb:*
> *half is not enough,*
> *he will take all you have,*
> *all at once, for his store.*
> *He breaks down your door.*

I have dwelt on all this again and again: this conflict, death and life, might and love, self-interest and welfare, this struggle of opposites to which only man's religious instinct can glimpse a true solution – a solution that is supreme peace, supreme good and supreme unity. Some passages could be cited from my Santi-niketan talks. But where I have made a confessedly religious expo-sition I may not have spoken my innermost truths; it is not unlikely that I have traded in truisms acquired from hearsay. In a literary work the author's purer being reveals itself uncon-sciously; the work thereby is a purer thing. That is why I go to poetry and drama for evidence.

In order to know life as real one has to make its acquaintance through death. The person who fearfully shies away from death and clings to life has not found life's essence, because he has no true respect for it. And so even while he is within the orbit of life he is constantly stalked by the horror of death. The person who rushes ahead to take death a captive can see that what he seizes on is not death at all, it is life. When I can't face it with courage, I see its shadow behind me. I look at that and perish every second. When I stand before it without fear I find that the same chieftain who leads us on the paths of life carries us through the portal of death. The opening scene of *Phalguni* is of young men out to celebrate the Spring festival. But this festival is no mere jolli-fication; it is not an occasion to be kept in a casual manner. Through the fatigue of decrepitude and the fear of death one arrives at the joy of new life. So the young men say, "We'll truss up Decay, that old creature, we'll take Death prisoner." We see this mirth and play and this Spring festival again and again in human history. As senescence deepens in social life, and custom becomes useless, and the torture imposed by old and outdated forms strikes at young life and saps its vitality, this is the time when man hurtles himself at death and through revolution and upheaval prepares for the festival of the new Spring. This pre-paration is in fact going on in Europe. There the festival of the Spring colours of a new age has begun. Human history has issued a summons to death because it has to reveal its own ever-young immortal form; and it is Death that has been engaged in beautifying it. So the Baul says in *Phalguni* —

"Age after age Man has fought, today the Spring wind brings the waves of that struggle. ... Those who are immortal through death have sent letters in the young leaves of Spring. They are calling out on all sides, 'We haven't quibbled about the way to take, we haven't grudged the fare, we came rushing onward to burst out in bloom. If we stopped to think, what would have happened to the Spring?'"

The letter I read in the young leaves of Spring, who wrote it? The very leaves that have withered and fallen have sent their message through death. If they could have clung to the branches, it is decrepitude that would have been immortal – and the cotton paper of old manuscripts would have made the whole forest yellow, and the sky would have shivered with the rustling of dry leaves. But the old expresses through death its eternal youth and freshness, and this is the true festival of Spring. So Spring says that those who fear death do not know life; they embrace decay and exist in a living death, cut off from the life-rich universe. –

CHANDRAHAS: Oh it's you... our captain. ... Where's the old man?

CAPTAIN: He's nowhere at all.

CHANDRAHAS: Nowhere? ... Then what is he?

CAPTAIN: He's a dream.

CHANDRAHAS: Then you are permanent?

CAPTAIN: Yes.

CHANDRAHAS: And we here are permanent?

CAPTAIN: Yes.

CHANDRAHAS: Those who have seen you from the back – in how many different ways have they thought of you? ... You certainly seemed very old at that time. Then you came out of the cave. Now you look like a boy. It's as if I'm seeing you for the first time! Again and again you are new, every time you are new. It's so strange!

(from *Phalguni*)

Man longs to experience life in a truer, larger, fresher way. The life that is continually in blossom in the journey of human civilisation, is so by continually conquering death. Man has said —

> *Again and again to death succumb,*
> *in order death to overcome.*
> *Only later life will come,*
> >*itself to take the throne.*

Man has learned —

> *It is no playful thing*
> *that all life through links me to you*
> >*each dawn, each evening.*
> *How often has the lamp gone out,*
> *with night's storm thundering all about,*
> *as you rock with uncertainty*
> >*the world's great swing!*
> *Again, again the dam gives way,*
> *the flood has come, this awful day*
> *fills all around with the dread sound*
> >*of suffering.*
> *O terrible one, I can expect*
> *blows from your love, not neglect.*
> *This word my grief, my joy has heard*
> >*in my heart ring.*

What is my religion? Even today I cannot say I know perfectly and clearly what it is — after all it is not a scriptural creed laid out in tenets and postulates. To know and look at this religion by uprooting it from the innermost tissue of life, by exposing it and holding it up for scrutiny, is not possible for me. But I know this for certain, that enjoyment of a lazy tranquillity and beauty is not the main purpose or ingredient of this religion. I admit, *anandaddhyeva khalwimani bhutani jayante,* "it is from *ananda* (joy) that all that exist are born"; and, *anandam prayanti abhisamvishanti*, "to *ananda* all depart and are withdrawn". But this is no joy that rejects sorrow, this is a joy that welcomes it. What is good in this joy is manifested by overcoming evil, not by rejecting it; what is immutable and absolute in it is gained by resolving division and conflict, not by ignoring them.

> *From its source of darkness coursing bright,*
> > *it is your light.*
> *Waking at conflict, not to be withstood,*
> > *it is your good.*
> *Scattered and spread in the dust of the road*
> > *is your abode.*
> *Made deathless in war's shove, its counter-shove —*
> > *is your dire love.*
> *When all is done with, what unseen is left*
> > *remains your gift.*
> *Carried by Death in brimming cup, past strife,*
> > *is all your life.*
> *Under humanity's feet as dust it's found,*
> > *your own true ground.*
> *To take all, hide in all is your design:*
> > *that you is mine.*

Satyam jnanam anantam. Shantam shivam advaitam. "Truth is endless knowledge. Peace is absolute good." In Hebrew mythology it is said that once Man lived in a world of immortality. That place was Paradise. There was neither sorrow nor death in that world. But if a heaven has not been obtained through sorrow and the battle with evil, it is not a heaven of knowledge – we do not recognise it as heaven at all. Just so a child in the womb does not know its mother, but knows her only through separation.

> *Leaving the mother's womb, her sphere,*
> > *and falling clear,*
> *soon the child its mother's form can see.*

With your embrace surrounding me,
in the cord wound, your form I do not know.
I fight, pound blow on blow:
when you expel me from your guarding-base,
I am aware, in my new separate place –
and see your face.

So it was that knowledge appeared in that paradise of unaware-
ness. And with the advent of knowledge a contradiction broke
out inside reality. The conflict of truth and falsehood, good and
evil, life and death took man out of heaven and exiled him in the
midst of shame and sorrow and pain. Passing through this
conflict man returns to the unfragmented truth from which he
shall not fall again. But where can the warring of all these opposites be resolved? In the infinite. So it has been said in the
Upanishads, *satyam jnanam anantam.* "Truth is endless knowledge." In the beginning man resides together with everything
animate and inanimate in the lap of the truth; knowledge brings
conflict and wins man to his freedom; and at last in the field of
consummate and infinite forms of truth it unites him with all else.
In the early condition of religious instinct there is the *shantam*,
"the Tranquil": man is then under the dominion of his own
nature. At this stage he wants only happiness and wealth, and like
a child thirsts only for pleasure, for his aim is gratification. After
that with the awakening of his humanity comes his dilemma.
Then he looks for a resolution of the duality of happiness and
sorrow, good and evil – then he does not evade sorrow and does
not fear death. At this stage there is the *shivam*, "the True and
Real", and the good is his aim. But this is not the end of it – the
end of it is in love, in joy. There like the confluence of the Ganga
and the Yamuna happiness and sorrow, enjoyment and renunciation, life and death commingle. There is the *advaitam*, "the One
and Absolute". There it is not merely the crossing of the sea of
separation and conflict; there it is the coming from the boat to the

shore. The joy that is there lies not at all in the absolute cessation of sorrow, but in the absolute consummation thereof. In this odyssey of the religious instinct life comes first, then death, then immortality. Man has obtained the right to that immortality. For among all animate beings only man has acknowledged sorrow and death on the perilous razor's-edge path of the good. Like Savitri he has reclaimed his own truth from the hands of Yama. He has come down from heaven to the ground of the mortal world; and so is able to embrace the world of immortality. It is only religion that drives man on past the typhoon of conflict to the shore of the One and Absolute, immortality, joy, love. How will those who see freedom in flying from the typhoon cross to the shore? That is why man's prayer is: *Asato ma sadgamaya, tamaso ma jyotirgamaya, mrityormamritam gamaya.* "From the unreal to the real, from darkness to radiance, from death to immortality lead me." The word *gamaya* signifies that we have to make our way along the path, that there is no avoiding it.

If there is any religious theory in my writings then it is this. Religious consciousness is in the apprehension of the relation of complete love between the animal soul and the divine and absolute soul, the love that has duality on one side and unity on the other. It has separation on one side and union on the other, bondage on one side and liberation on the other. Within this love prowess and beauty, form and taste, finite and infinite have become one. It is by accepting the universe that this love truly transcends it; and in acknowledging the past of the universe, it truly welcomes it. This love recognises peace (*shantam*) even in the midst of war, even in the midst of evil it knows good, and it worships the One even in the midst of the Many. The song of welcome that my religion sings is this –

> You have broken the door, you are here in radiant glow,
> yours be victory.

This noblest advent makes the darkness go,
yours be victory.
Triumphant hero, now at life's new dawn,
the scimitar of hope by your hand borne,
you smite that old confusion all outworn.
From chains release, set free.
Yours be victory.
Come cruel one, intolerable, even so
yours be victory.
Come fearless one, who no blemish know,
yours be victory.
O sun of dawn, in frightening attire
you come, and on the path of sorrow dire
your bugle sounds. In my soul blaʒe your fire.
Let death take heel and flee.
Yours be victory.

Ashwin–Kartik 1324

(Mid-September to mid-November 1917)

4

IT IS NOT EASY to acquire a true self-knowledge. The central thread of unity within life's diverse experience does not easily reveal itself. If the Creator had not given me a long life, if I had not been afforded the latitude of a seventy-year span, I would have lacked the opportunity to form a clear estimate of myself. I have looked at myself in many fragments, I have motivated myself in a number of areas of activity; and in this way again and again tokens of my identity have been scattered before me. Now I have followed this long orbit of life I can take a look at the circle in its entirety at the hour of farewell, and I understand that I have only one identity, and it is this: I am simply a poet. Again and again in my works my soul has let itself be seen by many; but the complete picture is not drawn there. I am not a guru versed in theory and scripture; nor am I a leader. Once I wrote, *I do not yearn to trumpet in / a new Bengal's new morning*, and I meant what I said. The messengers of spotless virtue cleanse the world of its sins, and make man take a vow of pure and healthy deeds – I revere them, but my seat happens to be some distance from theirs. But when that one pure radiance becomes varied and many, giving itself out in rays of many hues and colours to the world, I proclaim the many-hued One. We dance and make others dance, we laugh and make others laugh, we sing, we paint pictures – we herald the genius of variety (*avih*), that is excited in an unaccountable joy of cosmic manifestation. To assimilate the play of diversity within my soul, and to give it a playful external expression, is my work. I have no claim in guiding man to his goal; to travel in step with wayfarers is all my occupation.

The shadows on either side of the path, the wealth of green, the flowers and leaves, the song of the birds – it is to contribute to this fare of joy that we exist. The diverse and many-sided One who everywhere plays his game, in music and song, in dance and painting, in colours and shades, in forms and expressions, in the stress and blows of happiness and sorrow, in the struggle of good and evil – I have taken up the burden of his diverse sport, it lies with me to pick up and arrange the varied allegories of his theatre, this is my true self. People have given me other descriptions too – some have called me a theoretician, others have installed me as a schoolmaster. But right from childhood I have avoided the schoolmaster in my passion for play and play alone, and so the pedagogue's position is not mine. I recall the day when I came out, still a boy, with a flute in my hand, a flute of many openings and a hundred melodies, and the clear began to emerge from the unclear at the hour of dawn. It was the moment when darkness exchanged its first loving glance with light. Dawn's flood of messages overwhelmed its first barrier in my mind that day; the mind's lake danced and swung. Whether I grasped the meaning properly or not, whether I could speak of it or not, at the impact of that message further messages awoke in me. With so much at play in the universe in song upon song, there is a restlessness deep in the cosmic soul; and touched by its wave the soul of a boy was restless too, and still it has no rest. Seventy years are over, and even today my friends remonstrate with me upon my levity, and often there is a lapse in my seriousness. But there is no end to Vishwakarma's instructions. For he is frivolous, in the ceaseless winds of Spring playing in the woods he throbs with life for ever. And after all I cannot afford to waste my days encircled by a moat of seriousness. I have tried many paths these seventy years, and today I am in no doubt that I am the playmate of that restless spirit. I don't know what I have done, and what I shall be able to leave behind. I shall not sue for permanence. He plays but without attachment – the playhouse he builds he knocks down with his own hands. Yesterday evening in this mango-grove coloured designs were drawn that the Restless One has washed and wiped away in a night's storm, to be drawn afresh. If I have supplied a few toys in his playhouse I do not expect Time to make a collection of them. Broken toys will finish up on a heap of refuse. If I have filled with the sap of joy an earthen cup as small as the scrap of time that is mine, it is enough. Tomorrow the sap will run out, the cup will break, but the feast will not go bankrupt for that. Today as I turn seventy, in the name of the One who is all *rasa* I declare, as to my being greater or smaller than another, enjoyment of the game is spoiled by such a futile quibble. Assessors mill and squabble, yardsticks in hand; they must be ignored. I do not want to scramble and snatch at the chance bits of cheap fame that roll in the dust in a world of crowds. Let me never surrender to the temptation of a loud-voiced haggling over fees.

Even in this *ashrama* only what is concerned with expression is mine; its machinery is attended to by experts. I wanted to give shape to man's desire for self-expression. That is why I sought a hermitage to provide a background of form and beauty. Not in a city's brick and stone but in this arena of blue sky, the sunrise and sunset, I wanted to be the playmate of these innocent and lovely boys and girls. It is my part to assist in the good and beautiful flowering of a living union of souls in this *ashrama*. I have introduced other projects and my heart goes out to them where they find shape and beauty; yet my true and lasting place is not with them. Where the inchoate feelings of the village yearn for utterance I am there. The class I have started here for children is not the all and sum. My effort is to release the first emerging form of the tender lives of children in the playfield of Nature, to allow the radiance of the morning sun into the early days of their scholastic enterprise, to make room for the newly-burst bud of their striving. Otherwise I should have been lost in a jungle of rules and syllabuses. That work is secondary and external, my friends can take care of it. But allowing these children to dance and sing to the rhythm of the game of the Playful One, and occasionally giving them a holiday, to make their souls awaken in joy, is my own joy and my fulfilment. I am incapable of anything more serious than that. To those who would seat me on a platform to the sound of conch-shells I say that I was born for a lower position, that the Games Master has spared me from having to occupy the seat of the chief and veteran. Here I came and I poured out my heart over the dust and ground and grass, over the herbs and the ancient trees. Those who are close to the lap of the earth, those who are bred and raised by the earth, those who take their first steps on the earth and their rest on it at the end, I am a friend of them all, I am a poet.

Santiniketan
25 Baishakh 1338

(The date is Tagore's 70th birthday, 7 May 1931)

5

THE WORLD IN WHICH I first opened my eyes was something of a retreat. It was like a city's outskirts where the sky has not been choked up by neighbours' hubbub and houses on all sides.

Even before I was born our family had raised the social anchor and drifted far away from conventional moorings. Codes and regulations and rituals played little part in it.

We had a large old-fashioned mansion with a portico hung with a few broken shields and spears and rusted swords, and a prayer-hall, three or four courtyards, a front and back garden, and dark rooms stacked with fat drums for storing Ganga water the year round. The sequence of the various festivals of yester-year had once passed to and fro through the house with their many noises and decorations. I find myself outside the compass of their memories. I arrived when the old time had just retreated from this house and a new age had barely descended, its furniture yet to come.

Just as the current of this country's social life had shifted its course further away from this house, so had the tide of our former wealth begun to ebb. The lamps of Grandfather's wealth had shone out once with their many flames, but now the black stains of their burning-out were all that remained, and ashes, and a single feeble trembling flame. Even if the appurtenances of merry-making and enjoyment and luxury lingered in nooks and crannies, covered in dust and dirt and disrepair, left over from a past cluttered with things of comfort, no true sense of them remained. I was not born in riches, nor in the memory thereof.

The uniqueness that arose in the family in its isolation was natural, like the uniqueness of the flora and fauna of an island cut off and isolated from a continent. So there was a characteristic style to our language which people in Calcutta archly referred to as "Tagore-speak". And the same thing happened with the dress of our men and women, and also their manners.

At that time the élite of Calcutta had relegated the Bengali language to the women's house-bound world; only English was used in public life – in correspondence, in education, even in everyday speech. In our house this aberration could not happen. Love for the Bengali language ran very deep, and it was used for everything.

There was another noteworthy meeting of themes in the house. Through the Upanishads the family had an intimate relationship with India of the pre-Puranic era. Even when very young we used to recite *slokas* from the Upanishads nearly every day, on and on, pronouncing them flawlessly. From this it will be understood that the emotional effusion that is generally to be noted in the religious tradition of Bengal did not enter our house. The prayers introduced by my father were calm and composed.

This was one side of things; on the other the delight taken in English literature by my elders was profound. The atmosphere of the home thrilled to the enjoyment of Shakespeare's dramas, and Sir Walter Scott shed a powerful influence. At that time the country at large lacked all trace of patriotic zealotry. In poems like Rangalal's "Who wants to live in the absence of freedom?" and later in Hemchandra's "Where two hundred million live" one could hear the strains of yearning for the nation's freedom, like the song and chatter of birds at dawn. In the deliberations and arrangements for the Hindu Mela everybody in the family was active and enthusiastic, with Nabagopal Mitra as its central figure. The songs of this festival were "Victory to India" composed by my second brother, "How shall I sing India's praise in shame?" by my cousin Ganendranath, and "India, your face as the moon is wan" by my eldest brother. My elder brother Jyotirindranath had started a secret society that met in an abandoned derelict house and held its sessions amidst a display of Rig-Veda manuscripts, human skulls and bare swords, with Rajnarain Bose as the priest. It was there that we were initiated into the task of rescuing India.

This yearning and bustle and keen preparation did not take place in the press and throng of people. In peace and quiet its influence slowly penetrated our souls. Government policemen must have been either not alert or indifferent at the time; for they came to break neither our members' skulls nor the spell of their enjoyment.

The breast of the city of Calcutta was yet to be paved in stone; a great deal was simply bare. Smoke from oil-mills had not yet blackened the face of the sky. Through gaps in the forest of buildings sunlight shimmered on water in the ponds; *ashwattha*-trees cast a longer shadow in the afternoons; leaf-fringes of coconut-palms swung in the breeze; along a stone drain the Ganga's water fell like a fountain into the pond in our south garden. At times one could hear palanquin-bearers gasping and grunting in the lane, and from the main road came the cries of coachmen clearing the way. An oil-lamp burned in the evenings, and squatting on a mat by its faint light we would listen to the old maidservant telling fairy-tales. In this half-silent world I was a creature of the corner, shy, unboisterous, quiet.

For yet another reason I was something of an oddity. I was a truant from school, I did not take examinations, I did not pass them; my teachers lost all hope for my future. To the untrammelled respite that lies outside the classroom my mind turned like a refugee.

Meanwhile I had suddenly discovered under assurance from somebody, that the rhymes in metre that people called poetry were written with ordinary pens by ordinary mortals. That was a time when people who could make rhymes were looked upon with amazement. Now it is those who cannot who are regarded as extraordinary. In the province of *payar* and *tripadi* I went mad in the inexhaustible eagerness of my unhindered literary authority. With any number of divisions of eight and six and ten syllables, I busied myself in a corner in my game of making and breaking metre. Gradually the results saw the light of day.

Whatever the quality of those scribblings, there was a background to them: a boy who was shy and kept to himself, a loner, playing his own solitary games. He was beyond the reach of the constraints of society and outside the discipline of school. His household restrictions were few. Father was in the Himalayas; at home authority fell to the elder brothers. My brother Jyotirindranath, whom I most obeyed, imposed no restrictions on me. I used to argue with him and discuss this and that as if we were the same age. He knew how to respect a youngster. He aided my intellectual development by giving me mental freedom. If he had tyrannised me in a zest to dominate I might have twisted and turned myself into something – it might have been something acceptable to polite society, but not at all something like myself.

With this began a phase of poetic fragments in broken rhyme, like meteoric showers; it was a rough-and-ready, unreliable base for a boy's diffuse emotions. An inclination for breaking convention lay in the bones of this isolated child. There was considerable risk in this. But even here I avoided disaster. This was because at that time the crowd in the market-place of fame in Bengali literature was very small, fortunately for me – the excitement of competition was not yet at fever pitch. The rod of justice often rained down unpleasant blows of censure, but the turmoil of abuse and scandal had not yet soured the world of letters.

Of the few writers of the day I was the youngest and the least advanced in learning. My rhyme and metre were not reined in, my themes were befogged by inarticulate expression, an immaturity of language and feeling showed at every step. The littérateurs of the time rarely indulged me in their remarks or writings – rather they laughed a good deal at my gabble and babble. This was not a contemptuous laughter, not part of the trade in backbiting. There was reproof in their writing, but not the least trace of discourtesy. No malice showed even where disapproval was apparent. And so regardless of the lack of indulgence on my behalf, and of the contrary fashions of the time, I was able to develop my own writing in my own manner and way.

The first tranquil hour of obscurity passed away. I had been resting in the deep shadow of Nature's tender care and of my relatives' affection. Sometimes I would spend my time at the corner of the third-storey roof, weaving a garland of daydreams in an idle hour. Or I would sit under an old *neem*-tree in Ghazipur, and listening to the plaintive strain of water pumped out of a well to refresh a garden, I would set adrift on the Ganga as it flowed nearby my fancies laden with an unaccountable pain. Little did I know that from the light and shade of my own mind I would ever have to strike out on the high road of endurance, under a battery of prods and jabs from other minds. In the end fame arrived and dragged me out into the glare of the midday sun. The heat came gradually, the shelter of my corner crumbled away. The filth that comes with fame was far more of a defilement in my case than with others. No other writer had to put up with such relentless, such unreserved, such merciless, such unopposed denunciation. It is indeed a good yardstick of the extent of my fame. I have had reason to say that in the test of adversity fate has harassed me, yet not shamed me with the disgrace of defeat. Apart from this, out in the foreground of the black curtain that my unlucky star had hung for me, the beaming faces of my friends shone with radiance. That they were never few in number is apparent to me from today's meeting. I know some of my friends, and many of them I don't know, but these are the people from near and far who have communed with me at this festival – I am overwhelmed by their enthusiasm. Now I have a feeling they have come to see me off at the *ghat* – my ferry will start on a journey beyond daylight with their blessing ringing in my ears.

In the dusk of seventy years the journey of my days arrives at an epilogue. Before the light has all faded away my country shall have acknowledged the value of my long life in these anniversary celebrations.

As long as the crop is in the field there is uncertainty. Looking at the field the wise moneylender is wary of loaning too early, and keeps his main capital for himself. It is only when the crop is cut and stored that the price can be fixed according to weight. It seems that today I am at the post-harvest hour of reckoning.

The man who has lived long is as good as the past itself. It is clear to me that there is a certain distance between my eternal present and my contemporary present. On the very eve of my departure I stand near the courtyard of the poets who are already in the other world, having taken their turn in this. The indistinctness with which one is seen, carried as one is at the full pace of the chariot of the present, in my case should have passed by this time. From the foreground of the modern I have receded exactly to the distance to be attained to present a full view of life to the camera of the imagination.

Manu prescribed retirement to the forest (*vanaprastha*) after fifty. That is because according to Manu's reckoning after fifty one falls behind the present. For at that age the fatigue of determinedly keeping up with the race of time is greater than the satisfaction it affords; one is less revived, more exhausted. From that age therefore one has to urge oneself to row in the direction of that eternal estuary where Time is still. Having completed the *sadhana* of motion it is now time for the *sadhana* of stillness.

It is quite impossible in this age to adhere strictly to Manu's timetable. In his time there were certainly fewer responsibilities in life than now, and fewer entanglements. Nowadays education, work, even games or entertainment, whatever it is, has become a massive affair. However spectacular the emperor's chariot may have been at that time, it was simpler than the conglomeration of coaches to be found in the present-day railway train. It takes quite some time for a train-wagon to empty itself. The office closes at five by divine law, but before the files and ledgers are shut away and one heaves a sigh and sets off home, the lamps have to be lit. That is how it is with us. So unless the retiring age of fifty is extended we cannot take leave. But for one in his seventies there can be no excuse. From external evidence it is plain my time has run on ahead of me – at the very least I am already ten years behind. I am like the light from a distant star, a light that belongs to a previous time.

Before coming to a complete halt, however, due to the pace of moving forward, something of the backlash of the past must fall upon the present. When the entire song has run through all its notes it is really at an end, yet for some little time requests are made for an encore. It is merely a repetition of the past. One or two notes at the most may be added; but nothing is lost even if the singer keeps quiet. To try to keep repetition fresh a long time is like trying to keep a *koi*-fish alive out of water for about a month.

Let us extend this parallel a little between the fish and the poet. As long as the fish is in water it is worth supplying it with a small ration of food in its own interest. Later, when it is taken out of water, the interest turns out to be on behalf of some other animal. In the same way it is good to throw titbits of encouragement to a poet till he is past a certain point of maturity – that's in the interest of the poet. Thereafter, when his mature years are visited by the repose of reaching an end, if there is any need for the poet it is not in his own interest but in that of his country.

A country is the creation of man. A country is not all land but all soul. It is only when its people are expressive that a country is fully expressed. The more ringingly we assert the nobility of the motherland, sweet-watered, full-fruited, cool-blowing, the more we shall face the need for justification. It will be asked – if the gifts of Nature are merely material ingredients, how can they be brought to bear on the development of human excellence? If all the water in the land dries up through the intrusion of man, if the fruit dies, if the wind is poisoned by the germs of pestilence, if farmed land becomes barren, no amount of poetry will be able to hide the land's shame. The country is not made of land, it is made of people.

So in order to prove herself, the country is always waiting for those who have excelled in some pursuit. Even without them the flora and fauna will be born, the rain will fall, the rivers will flow, but the country will remain hidden like earth beneath the desert sand.

For this reason the country will seek occasion to recognise in public as her own one in whom she perceives an eloquent expression of herself. When this takes place, the day a person is gladly acknowledged by her is the day the person is born from the lap of the earth, to nestle in the lap of the country.

In the final phase of my life, if there be any truth in these anniversary celebrations, this is their significance. If in acknowledging me the country has not made any kind of discovery about itself, today's function must be futile. If anyone suspects the presence of pride and vanity in all this and is worried about me, I should say that his worries are unnecessary. The greater the display of a reputation whose capital is limited, the faster it goes bankrupt. The mistake appears to be a catastrophic one; in the end something trivial is left. The cloud-piercing light of the firework is also the brilliant signal of its extinction.

There can be no doubt that the country may be mistaken in selecting a recipient of its honour. The history of literature has often witnessed the silencing of the brief clamour of fame. So against the warning that one ought not to rejoice too much over the celebrations of the day, no argument will hold. Nor do I see good reason to be downcast at the present moment. From age to age the verdict of literary criticism undergoes reversal as well as restoration. If in the final judgement that is made by a fickle and sluggish time an absolute void be ordained one, there is no use fretting over it now. For the moment it is this function and immediate occasion that is my gain. Later on our great-grandchildren will be present for the final reckoning. For the time being let me rejoice contentedly in the company of friends; and may those otherwise disposed enjoy the thrill of puffing up the bubble to make it burst. In the black-and-white hues of these two opposing currents Yamuna, daughter of Yama, and Ganga, tumbling from Shiva's locks, mingle in the joyous river of the world. The peacock is pleased to dance in the pride of its tail, while the hunter is highly delighted to shoot it in the pride of his marksmanship.

In modern times in the West we see popular approval in regard to literature and artistic creation switching only too often. Speed increases in vehicles used by men; speed relentlessly drives at the hearts and minds of men.

Where worldly competition is severe this speed counts for a great deal. Where everyone scrambles after the windfalls of luck in the dust and throng of the market-place, the one who triumphs in speed is naturally the one who wins the game. Relentless speed is the vehicle of insatiable greed. The entire West is tottering like a drunkard in that greed. There increase of speed instead of being a means is gradually becoming an end in itself. It is the greed of speed that has burst out over water and land and sky today with an hysterical uproar.

But the substance of life is not an iron engine driven by the twin demons of steam and electricity. It has its own rhythm. It is a rhythm that can take on one or two extra measures, no more. One may move forward for a few minutes by turning somersaults, but before ten minutes are up it will be conclusively shown that human beings are not bicycle-wheels, their pedestrian gait falls in rhythm with the pace of the old poetic lyrics. The tempo of song is sweet when it obeys the living rhythm of the ear. If a double-quick measure is raised to a quadruple one, it is driven to leave the body of art, gasping to enter the body of inert technique. If you press for that extra measure, the *ragini* will beat its head on the main gate of the lunatic asylum and die. The living eye is not a camera, it takes time to have a good look at something. Looking on while going at a speed of twenty to twenty-five miles an hour is to subject it to a befogged view. There was a time when pilgrimage existed in our country as a living thing. It was undertaken with all the relish that travel can offer. In the age of the motor-car pilgrimage still remains, the journey does not, travel does not, arrival does — it is to pass an examination without learning anything, so to speak. In the works of the railway company capsules of pilgrimage are set out and offered at various prices, you can swallow any one of them — there is no pause in the process even to realise you have missed the real thing. If Kalidasa's *yaksha* had dismissed his cloud-messenger and sent an aeroplane-messenger to Alaka, then the *mandakranta* metre that fills up two cantos would have met with an accident after crossing a couple of *slokas*, and perished. Machine-made capsules of love's sweet absence (*viraha*) are yet to appear on the market.

Mighty people who are left untouched by the tragic climax of the poem *Meghadutam* ("Cloud-Messenger") are met with nowadays. Some say that the cry one hears in poetry now is a last laboured groan at its death. Its time is up. If that is true then it is not the fault of poetry, it is the fault of the time. The human soul is always attuned to a rhythm, but of late the time with its speeding engines has broken up its beat.

In a grape plot the farmer puts up sticks on the ground, and the grapevine creeps up the sticks to find shelter and bear fruit. In the same way some rules and regulations must be laid down to make life strong and successful. Many of these regulations are fence-posts of dull and lifeless advice and codes. But just as in a fence the posts of *jiol*-wood come to life as soon as the sap is found, so when life moves at a quiet pace to the rhythm of the soul, the dry fence-posts find the room to reach the inmost depths and begin to fill with life. It is in those depths that the sap of vitality lies. In that sap even such stuff as theories and principles comes to life and finds beauty as substance of the soul, and is touched with the hue of human joy. In the expression of this joy is eternity. The code of one day may not be accepted in the next, but the love and the beauty that this code has expressed in the true language of joy will remain new to us. The art of the Mughal Empire is fresh and young even today, whether we admire that empire and its policies or not.

But an age in which repose is cluttered and blocked with crowds of necessities and dulled by their pressure is an age of utility and not of love. Love takes time to deepen. In the modern age that is haunted by hurry the urge of necessity, like weeds of the water hyacinth, has made its way in countless forms even into the stream of literature. They do not come to live, they thrust themselves in with petitions for the solutions of problems in their hands. However flowery the petition may be it is not true literature, it is merely a petition. It vanishes as soon as the demand is satisfied.

In such a situation the literary climate changes by the hour. Nowhere does it leave its heart behind; at what it races past it kicks and spurns; on what it built high and towering, it heaps ridicule and scorn. The broad-bordered saris of our women, their *nilambaris* and Benares *chelis*, have remained unchanged on the whole for a long time – because they have owned the admiration of our heart. Our eyes do not tire of seeing them. They would indeed have tired if the mind, for lack of the repose in which to regard them with enjoyment, had turned insensitive and irreverent. In the set-up of a mindless and shallow luxury come the meaningless, facile, repeated turns and shifts of fashion. Present-day literature witnesses similar shifts in style and mode. In an unending race the heart cannot weave and tie the band of love and affection. Given enough time it would spin and weave the band with deep care. But busy people scold it, "Throw that beauty out!" Beauty is dated, beauty is old-fashioned. Get a roughly-wound hempen rope – let us call it Realism – that is what the racing-and-stumbling people of today would like. Ephemeral fashion is arrogant like an upstart nabob – its chief pride is that it is recent and contemporary, which means that it is proud of its time, not of its quality.

This motor engine of speed has its main station in the heart of the West. It is yet to become our own by an official deed. Yet our speed-race too has begun. We have jumped onto the footboard of their chariot that speeds like the wind. We too solemnly discuss the techniques of the latest fashion current in a short-haired and under-dressed literature; we too with the impertinence of the new take the greatest delight in defaming the old.

It was with all this in mind that I said that at my age I do not trust fame. To charge about in wild country in pursuit of this illusory deer is all very well for the young. For when one is young, even if the deer remains elusive the hunt itself is enough. The flower may or may not give fruit; yet in its restlessness the flower must give its own nature a ripe expression. It is disquieted; all the efforts of its colours and fragrance constantly open outwards. The work of the fruit itself is in the inner depths; its nature demands a modest and unruffled peace. Its striving is for emancipation from the branch, a freedom which comes in the wake of an inner maturity and fulfilment.

In my life today the season of fruit is come, a fruit that is eager for an early fall from the stalk. To enjoy this season's privilege fully, there has to be a mature reconciliation of the outside and the inside. That peace is devastated in the conflict of fame, obscurity and calumny.

Leave aside fame: the greater part of it is puffed up by the vapour of what is unreal. The man who feels excessively disturbed by its expansions and contractions is a wretched one. Love is the greatest blessing of fate, and it is also the best reward for a poet. He who can offer nothing but work may be repaid with fame, but the one whose burden it is to offer joy cannot be paid off without love as his due.

There are many achievements whose chief ingredient is Man. The state for instance. The power of action in it is in the number of people, which is why there is an incessant conflict to win people over to one side or the other. It involves spreading an extended net of fame in order to catch people. Think of Lloyd George. Only when a large number of people obey his intellect and submit to his power is his work done. With the slackening of trust the net tears, and the human ingredient begins to disappear.

On the other hand, if there is truth in the poet's creation the glory is in the creation itself, not in the approval of the populace. For it is quite common that such a creation meets with popular disapproval. That affects its market price but does not detract from its worth.

That the flower has bloomed is the highest message of the flower. The person who admires it is fulfilled, while the flower's triumph is in its own arrival. In the soul of beauty is a truth that is full of charm, bliss and mystery, and yet is beyond our reach; still it has an ineffable kinship with our own soul. Our awareness of it is deep and sweet and shining. Our inner being begins to grow, to quicken, to deepen in hue. Our being becomes one with it in colour and fragrance and sentiment – herein is a blossoming of love.

The poet's work is to rouse the human soul to this dawning awareness, and awaken it from indifference. He is considered a great poet who has made the human mind embrace things that are eternal, great, possessed of freedom, pervasive, profound. In the treasure-house of art and literature the gems of a people's aesthetic enjoyment are created and accumulated in every age and clime. In this wide world we can tell from literature alone to whom or to what the people of a country have given their love and admiration. Indeed it is by their love that we should judge people.

Many are the strings upon the *veena* of Veenapani, some of gold, some copper, some steel. Each tune that dwells in the throat of the cosmos, some light, some heavy, tunes of joy and enjoyment, all are played on her *veena*. In a poet's verse too is an endless variety of song. That every melody should ring with notes loud and high is not what I wish to say. And yet with each there should be a hint of the constant and eternal, of that sense of renunciation that purifies passionate attachment, and makes it virile and vigorous. In the poetry of Bhartrihari we see that the man given to the world of enjoyment has found his own song, but at the same time in the depths of his verse there sits the man of renunciation with his one-stringed instrument. It is in the collaboration of the two melodies that the balance is maintained, in poetry as in human life. Literature finds its true and permanent meaning by offering its gifts to distant times and various peoples; paper boats and clay pots cannot bear its cargo. Modernists may say with contempt that all this is out of tune with the lingo of modern times – if that is so we must feel sorry for the times. Our hope is that their span is not so long as to remain modern for ever.

If a wearied poet tends to feel that in the modern age the eternal themes of poetry are outdated, then the age must have grown old and insipid. His simple passion and enchantment does not reach out to the familiar world, and he is unable to welcome the world into his own soul. It is absurd to hope that an imagination that has ceased to find the vital sap in its vicinity will enliven any laboured composition for any length of time. When a palate is dulled it cannot relish the food that is eternal; and for the same reason it is scarcely possible that it will always find enjoyment in an item of outlandish cuisine.

Today in my seventieth year public knowledge of me has taken a certain shape. So I hope that those who have made the smallest attempt to understand me have finally gathered this: I was not born in a worn and withered world. What I saw on opening my eyes I never wearied of seeing, and I found no end or limit to wonder. My heart and soul have responded to the unarticulated message, the unstruck note that swirls about Creation and resonates from Time that has no beginning towards Time that has no end. I have felt as if I have heard this cosmic message for many ages. At a corner of the solar system the ethereal envoys of the seasons dress and decorate our small and green Earth in a variety of colours and sensations. I have never felt too lazy to join in the ceremony of this loving welcome with the offering of the water of coronation from my own heart. Every day at dawn I have stood in silence at the edge of the dark night only to comprehend the message in the words, *yatte rupam kalyanatamam tatte pashyami.* "You I behold in Your form most generous and pure." I have wanted to touch in my contemplation the great Being who is the principle of unity among the kinship of all beings, whose delight, manifest in countless forms, ceaselessly fills my soul with gladness in so many ways. My soul cries out, *kohyevanyat kah pranyat yadesha akasha anando na syat.* "Who will exhale and inhale if there is no joy in the sky?" It is this Being in whom the extraordinary phenomenon of the current of joy, that drives even what is absolutely useless, finds its deepest significance; this Being who is alive in the inner life of Man and constantly fulfils and enriches it. Because of this we cannot laugh at severe self-sacrifice and put it down to the suicidal madness of a lunatic –

> ... *for whom on night's dark stage*
> *Man the traveller moves from age to age.*

> ... *for whom a king's son wears*
> *his clothes in tatters, knows not the world's cares,*
> *begs in the street; and all vexations small,*
> *the horror beneath the ugly and banal,*
> *his great soul bears.*

93

... at whose feet honour's laid,
and wealth; for whom a hero's life is made
his sacrifice; for whom at a poet's hand
a thousand songs take breath from land to land.

The mantra from the *Ishopanishad* in which my father was initiated into the spiritual life has reverberated in my mind with ever-new significance, and I have said to myself again and again, *tena tyaktena bhunjithah, ma gridhah.* "Enjoy what He has scattered, give up greed." Delight in what has come to you freely; in what is about you lies eternity; do not give way to greed. In the *sadhana* of a poetic life this dictate is of immense value. The one who is caught up by narrow attachment like a spider in its web is left debilitated in the end; it brings mortification and weariness. For a narrow attachment uproots him from the whole and imprisons him within his own limits; after which he soon fades like a plucked flower. Great literature rescues enjoyment from greed, beauty from the passion of narrow attachment, the soul from the sentries of immediate demand. In the house of Ravana, Sita is imprisoned by greed and lust, in the house of Rama she is liberated by love, and there she is truly made known. The transcendental beauty of the body is revealed to love, to lust it is merely flesh.

I have been writing for some considerable time, at various phases and situations in life. I began at a callow age with no understanding of myself. So there is no doubt that my writing contains any amount of dross and excess. I hope that whatever is left over from all this lumber proclaims clearly that I have loved this world, that I have bowed to the Great One – I have longed for freedom in surrendering myself to the Perfect Being. I have believed that the truth of humanity is in the Great and Perfect One who is "ever immanent in every human heart", *sada jananam hridaye sannivishtah*. From the limits of the single-minded literary pursuit I had been accustomed to from childhood,

I ventured beyond at a certain point in time, to bring the offering of my work and the gift of my renunciation to that Great and Perfect One. If in this I have met with resistance from outside I have obtained solace and satisfaction from within. I am come to the great pilgrimage of this world. Here at the profound centre of the history of all lands, all nations and all ages is God-in-Man, at whose altar I have sat quietly and devoted myself to the arduous task of ridding my being of pride and ego and a habit of petty discrimination. It is a task that is not ended.

Notwithstanding whatever is trivial in me, if the innermost nature and *sadhana* of my character have come out in my writing and given happiness, I ask for love in return, and nothing more. I must be sure of this before I go, that I have received genuine friendship from those who in spite of my faults have known what I have longed for all my life, what I have received and given, what hints my unfulfilled life with its unfinished *sadhana* contains.

If a poet's true vocation is to create a treasure-trove of human delight in letters, then it is love alone that can receive the gift. Because it is love that takes an unfragmented view. To this day the work of those who are celebrated in literature we view as a whole and revere. We do not instinctively feel like tearing it to pieces, to find fault with and pick holes in. Such a great writer is yet to be born in this world whose best writing cannot possibly be lampooned, wilfully misinterpreted and indecently sneered at by any unappreciative creature with an ugly mind. The cheerfulness of love forms the simple background against which the poet's *œuvre* shines out in fullness and clarity.

I say in gratitude that I have received the highest blessing of the mortal world, love. I have received it from many of the great of the world – to them I offer not my thankfulness but my heart. At the touch of their generous right hand I felt on my forehead the touch of the greatness in Man – let whatever is best in me be worthy of their acceptance.

And my countrymen who have been able to love me through the haze of too much proximity and over-familiarity – in today's celebration their lovingly prepared offerings stand in splendid array. I receive this love of theirs with all my heart. –

> *Where life's road will lead when day has died*
> *is lost in the wild deep of darkness falling.*
> *Pointing to the way, all steady-eyed,*
> *"Fear not" stars are in their silence calling.*
> *Plucking the last flower of the tired day,*
> *I am going to end my journey's way,*
> *to find the shore of a new life's befalling.*
>
> *O my evening, all I had with me*
> *safe within your sari-hem is lying.*
> *Neighbour of night, a band-of-friendship see*
> *on your tender wrist of my hand's tying.*
> *What memories of joy, what dawn hopes thrill,*
> *what songs of dark, sweet griefs, are with me still,*
> *even at the time of life's farewell and flying!*
>
> *All that was mine, all that is over and done,*
> *falling behind as I go, itself so freeing,*
> *the beckoning gems – heart's racking storms – all gone*
> *to the horizon like a shadow fleeing,*
> *that wealth of life will not be cast away.*
> *In dark of dust's dishonour though it stay,*
> *it finds the touch of the feet of the All-Being.*

Poüs 1338

(Mid-December to mid-January, 1931-2)

6

THE MAIN INGREDIENTS that go to make up the body of a banyan-tree are no different from those that form the bodies of other lordly trees. The tree draws its own nourishment from the field that is common to all plants. For all those ingredients and items of nourishment we may appoint various names, and analyse them under different categories. But to the instinct and the inspiration that make a certain tree a banyan amid the infinite forms of plants, *tandurdarsham gurhamanupravishtam*, "the almost-never-seen being that is deeply rooted inside", to that invisible and profound essence what name can be given I do not know. It may be said that it is "the natural and spontaneous operation of its force", *swabhaviki balakriya*. This is not merely the instinct to articulate its personal and class identity, it is the instinct that continually evolves that identity. It pervades the entire being of a tree yet remains everywhere an elusive mystery. *Dhrajirekasya dadrishe na rupam*: the motion and work of that unique quality can be seen but its form stays hidden from view. Amidst unnumbered ways it secretly preserves its extraordinary individuality along a path of its own with perfect dexterity. It does not rest or go astray.

We do not readily think of this vibrant mystery deep inside us, but I have felt it again and again. Particularly as I stand today at the farthest end of life, my understanding of it is becoming increasingly clear.

Life's deepest meaning, its innermost truth, that is articulating itself in a gradual evolution outside, I can see as *pranasya pranam*, "life's living essence". I cannot claim it has found an easy path through me; there have been obstacles at every step. From the elements of the instrument of my life the Maestro has not been able to strike up his tunes as he would have wished. But I have understood the general character of his purpose in me. Distracted on all sides I have often misunderstood it, my attention has squandered itself down the wrong paths and ways, and sometimes perhaps the pride of excellence in other fields has deluded me. I have forgotten that according to one's inspiration the glory and worth of one's path is different for everyone. In my drama *Natir Puja* ("The Dancing-Girl's Worship") I tried to say this. The offering the dancing-girl wished to make to the Buddha was her dance. Other worshippers and ascetics had brought him gifts of their own innermost truth; the dancing-girl offered the finest and deepest truth of her life. And she proved the pure worth of this truth in her death. It was the living essence of her existence that awakened this dance in her heart and mind in its full splendour.

I have no doubt that within me a profound consciousness is guiding itself towards an unchanging creative goal, defying obstacles in its path as well as self-opposition. It is in the inspiration of this consciousness and in the vessel of this worship-offering that the homage of life can find a complete expression of its unity and individuality – if one is fortunate enough. Which is to say, if one's deep and esoteric instinct can find itself in positive harmony with one's situation and resources, if the distance between the musician and his music is lost in an immutable unity. Today as I look back I can trace from the outside the course of that supreme expression in the unity of my life's journey. At the same time I can realise within my soul that invisible Being at the centre of existence who in a purposeful sequence is weaving the data of life upon the thread of truth.

One has to look into the background of my life as it was in the context of our family. When I was born our home was not bounded on all sides by walls of the dead past of social customs that had more of habit in them than truth. The worship-hall of my ancestors lay empty in the house; of its rites and services I had not the slightest experience. Those secondary injunctions that are the troglodytes of sectarianism, those artificial codes and rituals by which the human intellect is confounded, which have for many centuries at different places and in the wildest forms led to the severest rifts between one nation and another, which have turned the degradation of mutual hatred and recrimination into a deep-seated and blind instinct, and the influence of which receded or lost some of its edge in all civilised societies at the end of the Middle Ages, but which have pervaded the whole of our national life and have emerged in ghastly conflicts in the state of our politics and society, of such practices and mores there was not a trace in either the inner or the outer orbit of our family. What I mean is that my soul and character in their shaping from birth were not overlaid by the scriptural tradition of a worn-out era. And in its act of new creation the power that shaped them did not have to keep a constant and watchful eye upon the raised finger of ancient instructions.

In the cosmic order of things is a marvellousness and all around is something that eludes our expression. No faith in ancient tradition, no special ceremonial rite has interfered with that feeling of wonder in my mind. There has always been a pure and unhindered communion between this world and my mind. From childhood I have found the deepest delight in the spectacle of the world. No worship can be simpler than this feeling of joy. Not from outside was I initiated in this worship; I have had to compose its mantras on my own.

The winter dawns of childhood are still bright in my mind. As the darkness of the nights paled I threw off my quilt and rose. At the eastern end of the walled garden of our estate the leafy fringes of a line of coconut-palms shimmered with the dew at that moment in the light of the young sun. Lest I be denied for a day the feast of this beauty I would put on a thin shirt, and with hands clenched tight before my chest I would defy the cold and rush out. Near the room to the north where the husking-pedal was stood an old hog-plum tree, and in another corner a *kul*-tree at the edge of a crumbling well – tempted by the unhealthy fruit, girls would crowd under it at noon. At the centre stood a stone trellis from an earlier age, streaked with moss and open crack-lines. And there was a large empty area, uncared-for and abandoned; and I cannot recall any other tree worthy of mention. This was my garden and this was enough for me. It was as if I was able to quench my thirst from a broken-rimmed vessel. A responsive soul within me secretly poured the water. All that I have had by way of material goods has been far exceeded by an inner delight and joy. Today I can see it was for this that I came to this world. I am not a holy man, not an ascetic. I have merely tasted the imperishable essence of the cosmos and returned again and again to say how good it was. When I came home from school in the afternoon, as soon as I got down from the carriage I looked up at the eastern sky above the third-storey roof, to see dark blue clouds in a thickened dense mass. In a moment a sense of wonder denser than the clouds would amass in my mind. On one side lay the distant sky softened by clouds, on the other a boy's heart thrilled with wonder, a boy who was a newcomer to this world. There was need for this amazing resonance for otherwise the metre would have lost its beat. The man of action is appealed to in the world; the onlooker at the side also is called upon. I have felt within me the passion constantly to satisfy the curiosity of idle gazing. This act of seeing is not merely a passive laziness. In the rhythm and beat of the seeing and the show is Creation.

There is an extraordinary statement in the Rig-Veda – *Abhra-trivyo anatwamanapirindra janusha sanadasi. Yudhedapitwa-michchhase.* – O Indra, you have no enemy, no hero and leader, no friend; yet at the moment of manifestation you desire friendship through communion (*yoga*).

However powerful one may be, in order to express oneself truly, one needs friendship and to be held dear by others. And there is so much in the universe to be held dear by the mind. So it is that song wakes from sound, and beauty and transcendence of form emerge from lines and curves. We seldom consider what a marvel this is.

I should say that this is my place in Creation, in this useless corner of the world. It is where I am called to. I have come to forge a bond with Indra, a bond of friendship. Life has among its necessities food and clothing and shelter, but none of the quality of joy and immortality. In this void the companions of Indra take their place.

> Anti santam na jahati
> anti santam na pashyati.
> Devasya pashya kavyam
> na mamara na jiryati.

He is near and cannot be parted from, he is near and cannot be seen. But look at that god's poetry, that does not wither or die.

The action and influence of the Creator upon beasts is close and direct. They are unable to withdraw from it and see Him. If He were linked to man only by system and process, then like the beasts man would have been stranded among the mere indispensable phenomena, and would not have found Him in consequence. But in the poetry of God it is through the ordered mesh of phenomena that the One who is beyond them all is manifest and apparent. That poetry comprises only His purest self-expression.

About this manifestation the sage has said —

> Avir vai nama devatar tenaste parivrita.
> Tasya rupeneme vriksha harita haritasrajah.

Avi is the name of this god; everything is suffused with him. All these trees — his form has made them green. He has set a garland of green about them.

The sage-poet saw the Poet's manifestation with a poetic eye. To explain the emergence of this Avi with his green garland, no reason can be cited that has its source in necessity. Nor can it be explained why he fills us with a delight that is the greatest reward of all. The animal in pursuit of a living has no claim on it. The sage-poet has said that the creator of the world made the cosmos with a half of himself. Thereafter the sage has asked, *tadasyard-ham katamah sa ketuh* – where and whither does the other half of him go? The answer to this question is well-known. Creation is manifest and visible; but beyond is a province neither manifest nor visible. Where would I have discovered its ineffable essence, had there not been that great respite beyond the piles of objects? It is here that the touch of what is uncreated falls on Creation, just as light descends on the Earth from the sky. In extreme fami-liarity we miss the poetry of Creation, for it exists beyond form and sound, where the Creator's other half is to be found, the half that is not imprisoned in matter. In this great area that lies beyond matter the union of hearts of Indra and his companions takes place. The lyre of all that is articulated sends out its message to that unexpressed world.

My days have gone by in all kinds of work, my mind has pur-sued attractions on every side. I have known the ways of the world and have had to submit to them. I have not been so obsessed as to allow my unbridled fancies to distort my view of them. But through all my interaction with the world my mind has escaped and found union in the area where Creation goes beyond Creation. In this union my life has found its fulfilment.

Once I said –

On this beautiful Earth I do not want to die.

The poet of the Rig-Veda has said –

Asunite punarasmasu chakshuh
punah pranamiha no dhehi bhogam.

Jyok pashyema suryamuchcharantam
anumate mrirhaya nah swasti.

Leader of Life, give me again eyes, give me again life, experience, enjoyment. I shall always behold the journeying sun,
give me contentment.

It is indeed an expression of friendship, when the friend's
manifestation has won the heart. Can there be a song of greater
praise? *Devasya pashya kavyam.* "Look at God's poetry." The
mind says, look at the poetry. The depth of the vision cannot be
fathomed.

Here it may be asked: Have I not been united with Him in my
work?

I have been, evidently. But it was not through work in a
machine-shop cluttered with wood and iron. Even as work it was
poetry. Once in Santiniketan I took the resolve of giving myself
over to education, and the field of my creativity as an educator
lay in the realm of the Creator's poetry. I called on the co-oper-
ation of the land and the water and the sky of this place. I wanted
to establish the pursuit of learning on the altar of delight. In
songs that heralded the seasons I awakened the minds of my
pupils to the carnival of Nature.

Here the principle of the spontaneous awakening of creativity
was immanent from the beginning. In the complete living thing
I had in mind I wanted to give the intellect an honoured place. So
in my field of work I have tried my best to allow science a
respectable position.

The Vedas say —

Yasmadrite na sidhyati yajno vipashchitashchana
sa dhinam yogaminwati.

Which means that the One without whom the worship and
sacrifice of even the greatest sages come to nought, is met with
through the mind and the intellect, not through the bond of the

mantras, nor through magical rites. And that is why I have always tried to harness the dual forces of intellect (*dhi*) and delight (*ananda*) in my creative work here.

On the one hand in this place I have called upon a joyous communion with Nature, and on the other I have earnestly wished to make the bond between man and man a bond of hearts. Where in the sphere of duty and work the bond of hearts becomes weak and narrow, form and custom grow supreme like a god. Instead of creativity it is the skill of building an assemblage that gains ascendancy. Gradually the contrivances of the mechanic win the right to disregard the poet's verse. The metre and diction within which the poet's literary work finds tongue is entirely under his own control. But where a work of creation involves many people it becomes impossible to preserve its purity. It is in such situations in human society that spiritual pursuit loses its freedom under sectarian legislation to become fossilised. I can only hope that the complex web of lifeless factional rules and stipulations shall not extinguish the vital principle of the *ashrama* in the future.

I do not know if there will be another occasion for it, and so standing as I do within the arena of a life of eighty years, I have resolved to introduce the truth of my life in a comprehensive way. But a perfect harmony of resolve and action is never possible. So one can look at oneself in terms of inner inspiration and instinct on the one hand, and outward momentum and motivation on the other. I have often referred to *tapovana* (the forest hermitage) as the *ashrama*'s model. I have received the notion of *tapovana* not from a survey of history but rather from poets and their verses. And naturally I have tried to realise and establish that ideal on a poetic scale. I have wished to say *pashya devasya kavyam* — as a human being, look at the divine poetry. I have chanted the Upanishads since childhood and my mind's inner eye has learnt to recognise by habit the fullness and splendour pervading the cosmos. This fullness is not material, it is spiritual; for it to be known the material burden has to be lightened. Those who saw me at this *ashrama* in its early stage most certainly know the idea and the form I had in mind. At that time its main feature was a lack of equipment and facilities. A simple way of life scattered everywhere the pure and clear quality of truth. In games, music and acting my relation with the boys opened out in an ever-new flowering of personality. It was easy to glimpse amidst my work the Peaceful, the Good and the Non-Dual Being (*shantam shivam advaitam*), whom I had called out to in the meditation of my heart. For the work was uncomplicated, the daily routine simple, the students few in number and most of the handful of teachers with me believed in the statement, *etasminnu khalu akshare akasha otashcha protashcha*: by that constant immutable Being the sky is held as the warp is to the weft. – They could utter with profound faith, *tamevaikam janatha atmanam*: know this Unique Being, know the all-pervading Soul, *atmanyeva*, in your own soul – not in traditional rites and ceremonies, but in love of humanity, in good deeds, not in being worldly-wise, but in the inspiration within. Through the poverty that attended our daily chores and duties in an atmosphere of spiritual reverence shone the life of patient renunciation.

One day when I was a boy the light of the morning sun ventured down what path of its rising I know not, and of a sudden illustrated all human relationship before me in the radiance of the soul. Although before very long the light was to vanish in the squalor of everyday life, still I hoped that one day before retiring from this world I would witness the whole of humanity illuminated by the light of that one soul. But at the summit of my inner awakening the path of that light's flow was obscured by fog and mist. Be that as it may, at least in the field of life's labours I have had the chance to reap a few treasures of joy. In the ground of worship and sacrifice that once I prepared in this *ashrama*, in the unassuming rites that were performed, I was able to offer hospitality to that greatness of the human spirit that has been greeted by the words *atithidevo bhava*, "be God as our guest." God is indeed in the guest. I cannot say that the pride of success never possessed my mind, but such weakness was overwhelmed and exceeded by the fulfilment of self-sacrifice. Here I have had the rare privilege of combining intellect with wisdom and judgement in a disinterested endeavour.

In welcoming all nations and races I have allowed no opportunity that might lead to the awakening of wisdom and judgement to pass by. Again and again I have yearned –

> *Ya ekohvarno bahudha shaktiyogat*
> *varnananekan nihitartho dadhati*
> *vichaiti chante vishwamadau sa devah*
> *sa no buddhya shubhaya samyunaktu.**

Santiniketan
1 Baishakh 1347

(14 April 1940. The first day of the year in the traditional Bengali calendar. Tagore died on 7 August 1941.)

* "May He who is non-dual and without various forms, who from some inscrutable purpose and by means of many forces has decreed at the beginning of Creation a multitude of forms, that shall fade away at the end of the cosmos and be reclaimed into Him, unite us to good sense and wisdom."

POEMS BY TAGORE QUOTED

Agaman (Arrival)
Antaryami (The All-Discerning Being)
Ashesh (The Endless)
Atmasamarpan (Self-Surrender)
Dan (The Gift)
Ebar Phirao More (Now Call Me Back)
Janmantar (Another Life)
Jibandebata (Life-God)
Jyoti (Radiance)
Kabicharit (A Poet's Biography)
Kalika (Bud)
Maranmilan (Death's Tryst)
Mukti (Liberation)
Prabasi (The Exile)
Pran (Life)
Varshashesh (Year's End)
Vasundhara (The Earth)
Vishwanritya (Cosmic Dance)

Prose quoted

Page *(a, b, c denote the first and subsequent quotations)*

59–60	Essay: Pagal, 1904 (The Mad Spirit)
23–24	Letter, 10 October 1895
29–30a	Letter, 14 June 1892
30b	Letter, 20 August 1892
30c–31	Letter, 9 December 1892
56–57	Letter, 5 October 1895

WORKS BY TAGORE QUOTED

(Established English titles are given where they exist)

POETRY

Balaka (A Flock of Geese), 1916
Chitra (The Colourful Enchantress), 1896
Gitali (Songs), 1914
Gitanjali (Song Offerings), 1910
Gitimalya (Song-Garland), 1914
Kalpana (Imagination), 1900
Kari o Komal (Sharps and Flats), 1886
Kheya (The Ferry), 1906
Kshanika (Instants), 1900
Naibedya (Offerings), 1901
Sonar Tari (The Golden Boat), 1894
Utsarga (Dedications), 1914; composed in part 1900–03

DRAMAS

Malini (Girl of the Gardens), 1896
Achalayatan (The Immovable), 1912
Natir Puja (The Dancing-Girl's Worship), 1926
Phalguni (Song of Spring), 1916
Prakritir Pratisodh (Nature's Revenge), 1884
Raja (The King of the Dark Chamber), 1910; reference only
Saradotsav (Autumn Festival), 1908; reference only

QUOTATIONS FROM TAGORE'S POETRY

I

3

QUOTATIONS FROM THE SANSKRIT

References for quotations from the Sanskrit are below. In a few cases Tagore includes a translation or close paraphrase in the Bengali; in all others (given in inverted commas in the text) the translators have rendered directly from the original Sanskrit. For a few words and phrases that are fairly common references are omitted. The mode of transliteration followed is the common one without diacritical marks, not the orthodox one.

3

52   *mahadbhayam vajramudyatam.* Katha Upanishad 2:3:2.

63   *Rudra yatte dakshinam mukham tena mam pahi nityam.* Swetaswatara Upanishad 4:21.

65   *durgam pathastat kavayo vadanti.* Katha Upanishad 1:3:14.

65   *nayamatma balahinena labhyah.* Mundaka Upanishad 3:2:4.

69   *anandaddhyeva khalwimani bhutani jayante* ... Taittiriya Upanishad 3:6.

69–70 *anandam prayanti abhisamvishanti.* Taittiriya Upanishad 3:6.

72   *Asato ma sadgamaya, tamaso ma jyotirgamaya, mrityormamritam gamaya.* Brihadaranyaka Upanishad 1:3:28.

5

93   *yatte rupam kalyanatamam tatte pashyami.* Isha Upanishad *sloka* 16.

93   *kohyevanyat kah pranyat yadesha akasha anando na syat.* Taittiriya Upanishad 2:7

94   *tena tyaktena bhunjithah, ma gridhah.* Isha Upanishad, *sloka* 1.

95   *sada jananam hridaye sannivishtah.* Swetaswatara Upanishad 4:17 and elsewhere.

6

Notes

Introduction

9   *Baul* Member of an unconventional, deeply-animated sect of singers and musicians in Bengal with a universal spiritual message.

11   *slokas* A *sloka* is a Sanskrit verse-unit.

I

18–19   *ragas, raginis* The *ragas* are the primary modes of Indian music and the *raginis* the variations from these.

21 ff   *Jibandebata* Literally "life-god". See Introduction p. 11 and excerpts from the poem of that name on pp. 25–27.

22   *Ashwin* Bengali month, mid-September to mid-October, in the season of autumn.

26   *veena* See note to p. 34.

27   *ghat* Steps leading down to a river; a boarding-place or a landing-place.

29   *veena* See note to p. 34.

29   *"with water channels ringed"* Tagore quotes the term *jalarekhavalayita* from his own letter dated October 5 1894. This compound word is his adaptation from the Sanskrit *mritpindo jalarekhaya valayitah* ("a ball of clay with water channels ringed") quoted from the *Vairagyashataka* of Bhartrihari (see note to p. 92) in the same letter.

34   *Vani* is Saraswati, the goddess of speech and learning, and poetry and music. She carries a *veena*, a traditional stringed instrument.

2

37   *Chitragupta's accounts office* Chitragupta is the registrar of Yama (the god of death) and recorder of the virtues and vices of mankind. After death one receives one's due according to the record.

38   *Manu* An early law-giver, who wrote the famous *Manusamhita* that codified Hindu law.

3

45   *a Vaishnavite, a Shakta* The Vaishnava and Shakta traditions of belief constitute the two main strands of Hinduism. Vishnu is above all the god of love. The Shakta believer worships Shiva and the idea of latent force (*shakti*) He embodies.

50   *Shiva ... poison* In legend gods and anti-gods churned the ocean. Much that was valuable came up, but also some terrible poison that threatened to destroy the world. Shiva, god of creation and destruction, drank the poison to save the world, holding it for ever in his throat, that turned blue as a result.

55   *veena* See note to p. 34.

58   *Bangadarshan* A pioneering literary periodical.

60   *Shambhu* is another name for Shiva, who is also celebrated as Nataraj, the King of Dance.

63   *Rudra* The Terrible One. A personification of the destructive aspect of the universe, often identified with Shiva.

64   *veena* See note to p. 34.

65–6   *Sudarshana, Subarna* In the drama *Raja* the queen Sudarshana values external beauty. The king rules with love and freedom, never tyranny. He is not externally handsome and meets with his queen only in darkness. When she insists on seeing him he asks her to try and recognise him in a festival throng. Mistakenly she picks out Subarna, a worthless handsome man posing as the king. ("Subarna" means gold.)

Now the king lets her see him. In shock she leaves him; seven other kings want to marry her; a war breaks out. Ultimately the good king's supremacy is established, almost self-evidently, and she comes back willingly.

67 *Santiniketan talks* These were morning talks on spiritual and philosophical issues that for some years Tagore gave in Santiniketan in Bengal.

67 *the festival of the Spring colours* This is *holi*, when Spring is celebrated by a joyful playing with coloured powders among family and friends.

67 *Baul* See note to p. 9. Tagore created the character of a blind Baul in *Phalguni* who sees with his heart and brings the tidings of Spring.

72 *Savitri* A famous character of mythology and an ideal of Indian womanhood. She married Satyavan knowing he would die after a year. On the day of his death she followed Yama, the god of death. Impressed by her devotion and power of reason he returned her husband to life.

73 *Kartik* Mid-October to mid-November.

4

76 *Vishwakarma* The heavenly architect in Hindu mythology. The unceasing lightness and new life in Nature shows that Vishwakarma's heart is ever-young, and that he expects the same of us.

77 *rasa* Literally sap or essence, the word is used in numerous derivative senses like joy, love, humour, the dominant mood of an artistic piece, and so on.

77 *ashrama* A hermitage, a place of contemplation and learning that in ancient India was situated in the forest. In the school he founded and taught at in Santiniketan Tagore revived the culture of holding classes in the open. His father had set up an *ashrama* at Santiniketan and Tagore continued to use the term for both the school and the place.

5

79   *a large old-fashioned mansion* This was the Tagore family home in Calcutta.

79   *Grandfather* Rabindranath's paternal grandfather, Dwarkanath Tagore (1794–1846). A glamorous personality, he was known for his vast business enterprises, his regal style of living, his interest in Indian social reform and his lavish charities. He visited England twice and died there.

80   *slokas* See note to p. 11.

80   *Rangalal, Hemchandra* Rangalal Bandyopadhyay (1827–87) and Hemchandra Bandyopadhyay (1838–1903) were famous poets who composed patriotic songs and played a part in the awakening of Indian nationalism.

80   *Hindu Mela* A fair first held in 1875 to celebrate the nationalist cause. Tagore's family lent their support and composed songs for it.

80   *Nabagopal Mitra* (1840–1904) was a leader of the nationalist movement in 19th-century Bengal. He was the guiding spirit behind the Hindu Mela and involved himself tirelessly in many cultural pursuits and forward-looking movements in society. He was a close friend of the Tagores.

81   *Rajnarain Bose* (1826–99) Writer, scholar, educationalist and public figure. A close friend of the Tagore family.

81   *ashwattha-trees* A large, spreading fig-tree, the pipal, sacred to Hindus and Buddhists.

82   *payar* A very popular metre in which each two lines rhyme and each line consists of fourteen letter-syllables.

82   *tripadi* A metrical scheme in which half-line triplets alternate in rhyme. An instance of this is the verse "Now cruel one", p. 55.

83   *neem-tree* An aromatic tree of bitter extract whose various products are much used.

83   *at this festival* The Poüs festival is a popular winter event in Santiniketan instituted by Tagore to commemorate the

induction into the Brahmo Samaj of his father, Maharshi Debendranath Tagore (1817–1905). This was a new religious movement (see Introduction). The Maharshi may be said to have given it its momentum.

84 *ghat* See note to p. 27.

84 *Manu* See note to p. 38.

84 *sadhana* The disciplined pursuit of a noble end.

85 *koi-fish* It lives longer out of water than do most fish species.

85 *sweet-watered, full-fruited, cool-blowing* A quotation from "Vande Mataram" (Hail Thee Mother), a song composed by Bankim Chandra Chatterjee in Sanskrit and Bengali that was a mantra for the Independence movement. It became India's national song. The Sanskrit words that are echoed are *sujalam suphalam malayajashitalam*.

87 *Yama* is the god of death; the river Yamuna is said to be his daughter. (Another tradition has them brother and sister.) The god Shiva bore down the great river Ganga (Ganges) from the heavens to Earth and let it escape through his hair as a favour to a legendary Earth-king.

88 *ragini* See note to pp. 18–19.

88 *Kalidasa* was one of the greatest Sanskrit poets and dramatists and *Meghadutam* ("Cloud-Messenger") is one of his most celebrated works. It is a long poem narrated by a *yaksha* (a member of a class of demi-gods) who has been punished by his King with a year-long banishment from Alaka, the capital of the Yaksha realm. He pines for his wife in Alaka and requests a cloud to take her a message of love. As he describes the route to the cloud, a vivid and beautiful description of rain-swept India emerges. It is written in the long and slow *mandakranta* metre. Kalidasa's dates are disputed but he may have lived in the fifth century A.D.

88 *slokas* See note to p. 11.

88 *jiol-wood* A wood that lasts longer than that of most trees.

89 *nilambaris* Blue saris, very popular in the Bengal of old.

89   *Benares chelis* Traditional headwear of a Bengali bride, made of a fine silk from Benares.

91   *Lloyd George* The British Prime Minister at the time of writing.

92   *veena* See note to p. 34.

92   *Veenapani* A name for Saraswati (see note to p. 34).

92   *Bhartrihari* was a Sanskrit poet and man of letters of the 6th to 7th century A.D. He alternated between a monastic and a worldly life.

92   *the man of renunciation with his one-stringed instrument* is a Baul (see note to p. 9).

94–95   *sadhana* See note to p. 84.

94   *Ravana, Sita, Rama* The main characters in the *Ramayana* epic, in which Ravana abducts Sita, the bride of the exiled prince Rama.

6

100   *kul-tree* A thorny tree bearing large edible sour berries.

100–2   *Indra* Indra is the king of the Vedic gods and the god of the sky and the thunder.

104–5   *ashrama* See note to p. 77.